Financial Management in Local Government

David Rawlinson and Brian Tanner

General Editors:
Michael Clarke and John Stewart

Second Edition

PITMAN
PUBLISHING

in association with the
Institute of Local Government Studies

PITMAN PUBLISHING
128 Long Acre, London WC2E 9AN
Tel: +44 (0)171 447 2000
Fax: +44 (0)171 240 5771

A Division of Pearson Professional Limited

© Longman Group UK Limited 1990
© Pearson Professional Limited 1996

First edition published by Longman Industry and Public Service Management
in 1990 under the title *Financial Management in the 1990s*
Second edition published by Pitman Publishing in 1996

The right of David Rawlinson and Brian Tanner to be identified as Authors
of this Work has been asserted by them in accordance
with the Copyright, Designs and Patents Act 1988

ISBN 0 273 62523 3

British Library Cataloguing in Publication Data
A CIP catalogue record for this book can be obtained from the British Library.

10 9 8 7 6 5 4 3 2 1

Typeset by Phoenix Photosetting, Chatham, Kent
Printed and bound in Great Britain by Redwood Books, Trowbridge, Wiltshire

The Publishers' policy is to use paper manufactured from sustainable forests.

Financial Management
in Local Governme·

Managing Local Government Series

Human Resource Management in Local Government (second edition)
by Alan Fowler

Performance Management in Local Government (second edition)
by Steve Rogers

Renewing Public Management: an agenda for local governance
by Michael Clarke

Shaping Organisational Cultures in Local Government
by Janet Newman

Understanding the Management of Local Government: its special purposes, conditions and tasks (second edition) by John Stewart

Contents

Dedication   vi

Editors' foreword   vii

Acknowledgements   ix

Abbreviations   x

Introduction   xi

1 Financial management in context   1

2 The chief financial officer's role   7

3 Decentralising financial management   18

4 Compulsory competitive tendering   26

5 Information technology   45

6 Financial management functions – exchequer   57

7 Financial management functions – co-ordination, control and accountability   72

8 Financial management functions – audit, commercial, information and advice   85

9 Progress in decentralising financial management   102

10 Towards the millennium   116

Appendices

A Summary of financial management functions   123

B The financing of local government   125

C The definition and control of capital expenditure   134

D Service level agreements and a framework for support services   141

Glossary of financial terms   146

Index   155

Dedication

This book is dedicated to the many colleagues and friends in Somerset County Council and Wolverhampton Metropolitan Borough Council whose expertise, commitment and good humour provided the inspiration for its creation and continued survival. They are in no way to blame for its inaccuracies or shortcomings.

Editors' foreword

This book is one of a series of management handbooks published by Pitman Publishing in association with the Institute of Local Government Studies in the School of Public Policy at the University of Birmingham. The series is designed to help those concerned with management in local government to meet the challenge of the late 1990s. It is based on the belief that no period has been so important for local authorities to have effective management, responsive to both citizen and customer.

The mid 1990s have brought reorganisation to local authorities in Scotland, Wales and parts of England. No local authority, however, can escape the need to keep under continuous review its political and managerial structures and processes. All councils are caught up in far-reaching changes. Some of these come from local determination and decision, others from central government policy and yet others from deeper changes in society. New problems, issues and opportunities demand from local governments a capacity to respond in new ways. They have to become closer to their local communities, their public and the wide range of institutions and organisations involved in the governance of localities; they need to find imaginative solutions to the ever more complex problems of public policy; they have to manage their resources to achieve value for money and value in the services they provide; and they have to achieve effective management in all their activities. These are formidable challenges for the managers – and the politicians – involved.

There are plenty of management books, but this series is distinct. Its starting point is the need for emphasis on developing effective management in local government, associated with the need to take account of the particular nature of local government. The series sets out to be succinct and to be useful in the practical day-to-day world as well as being designed to be used as a prompt to management improvement.

In no sense are we pretending that this or other books in the series will show a *single way* to manage the local authority. Management is not like that. Our intention is to explore ideas and questions in order to help fashion the most helpful and effective approach to the local situation. We believe that local authority politicians and managers should draw on as wide a range of experience as possible but that this should be set in the context of the special purposes, conditions and tasks of local government. We hope that this book contributes to that end.

Professor Michael Clarke, Head of School of Public Policy
University of Birmingham

Professor John Stewart, Institute of Local Government Studies
in the School of Public Policy, University of Birmingham

Acknowledgements

The revision of this book has been every bit as spontaneous as its creation. I am grateful to Wolverhampton Council for allowing me to undertake this task, and particularly to Roy Lockwood, Director of Education, and Brian Bailey, Director of Finance, for their support. I am also grateful to the Chartered Institute of Public Finance and Accountancy for allowing the reproduction of extracts from their Local Authority Finance Glossary. Special thanks once more to Jean Rawlinson, who carried out the major task of transferring the whole of the original manuscript on to a different computer system; without her efforts this new edition would not have been possible.

David Rawlinson

Abbreviations

Certain abbreviations appear regularly throughout this book. To save space and to assist readers from non-financial backgrounds, the full titles or terms are listed below. Where necessary, these terms are explained in the Glossary of financial terms at the end of the text.

ACG	Annual capital guideline
AVC	Additional voluntary contribution
BACS	Banks automated credit system
BCA	Basic credit approval
CCT	Compulsory competitive tendering
CIPFA	Chartered Institute of Public Finance and Accountancy
CFO	Chief financial officer (otherwise known as County/Borough/District Treasurer or Director of Finance)
DFEE	Department for Education and Employment
DLO	Direct labour organisation
DSO	Direct service organisation
DSS	Department of Social Security
ERDF	European Regional Development Fund
ESF	European Social Fund
EU	European Union
FIS	Financial information system
GEST	Grants for education support and training
GREA	Grant-related expenditure assessment
IT	Information technology
LEA	Local Education Authority
LMS	Local management of schools
PC	Personal computer
PWLB	Public Works Loan Board
RCCO	Revenue contribution to capital outlay
RER	Return of expenditure and rates
ROCE	Return on capital employed
RO/CO	Revenue out-turn/capital out-turn
RPI	Retail price index
RV	Rateable value
SLA	Service level agreement
SLS	Service level statement
SRB	Single regeneration budget
SSA	Standard spending assessment
SSP	Statutory sick pay
VFM	Value for money
ZBB	Zero-based budgeting

Introduction

Objectives

This book has evolved from an earlier publication entitled *Financial Management in the 1990s* which was commissioned in 1989. The initial brief we were given at that time was to write a book about financial management to be aimed specifically at non-finance managers. In other words it was intended to be a layman's guide to financial management in local authorities. After due reflection we considered that both the value and the lifespan of such a book would be limited because of the rapid pace of change in the local authority finance world.

We therefore decided to pursue twin objectives. As instructed we attempted to explain the role, functions and techniques of financial management in a way which would be helpful to non-finance managers. In addition, we attempted to 'gaze into the crystal ball'. We put forward a view of financial management in local government which we felt would be in tune with the requirements of the 1990s. This was very much our vision and we were conscious at the time that not only would there be many variations on our theme but also the theme itself might fail to emerge.

Five or so years on it is fair to say that our central prediction of a progressive decentralisation of financial management functions has not yet become a dominant theme of the 1990s. However, some of the variations on the theme which we explored five years ago e.g. service level agreements (SLAs), have become well established. In addition, many of the principles and problems which were highlighted at that time remain relevant and therefore feature again, particularly in Chapters 1 to 3.

Since the original version of this book was published, both authors have moved out of the Finance Department and, in one case, to another local authority. Consequently, this new edition has a distinct service focus, and may be less up to date in some of the technical aspects of financial management than its predecessor. Nevertheless the basic approach remains the same. Readers whose immediate or only objective is to discover what financial management is about should read Chapters 1, 6, 7 and 8 in full before using the summary sections at the start of the other chapters to identify issues of special interest. A glossary of financial terms has also been provided at the end of the book to assist the non-specialist. Those with financial management expertise who wish either to question our transience or to benefit from our experience should concentrate on Chapters 2, 9 and 10, and could well omit Chapters 6, 7 and 8 altogether.

It is important at this early stage to clarify our use of the term 'decentralisation' in the chapters which follow. We apply this term to any change which reduces the degree of centralised management control within a local authority, particularly in respect of the chief financial officer's (CFO) department. Decentralisation therefore encompasses both the delegation and devolution of specific functions. Our own distinction between these two terms is explained in Appendix D.

Finally by way of introduction we wish to stress once again that this book is not intended to be theoretical or academic. Neither is it intended to be a comprehensive text book on financial management. We have not even sought support for our views in existing published material and have not therefore provided a bibliography. This is a practical account of financial management in local government and a practitioner's view about where current developments might lead. It is intended:

- to help non-finance managers to understand the financial management processes within local government; and

- to give them and others a wider perspective of the developments in financial management which are under way, and their role in those developments.

The background

The 1990s have seen a succession of major upheavals in the sphere of local government finance. The most memorable of these was the poll tax experiment, but this has been rivalled by 'white collar' compulsory competitive tendering (CCT) and Local Government Review. Local management of schools (LMS) and community care have been marginally less controversial, but equally far reaching. The Citizens Charter has generated spasmodic public interest and the development of the 'bidding culture' has 'progressed' as far as the National Lottery.

These changes have imposed huge demands on local authorities in general and on finance departments in particular. At the same time, developments in information technology (IT) have presented new opportunities for solving the information and technical problems.

So far, the response by local authorities, in terms of structural change, has been less dramatic than we originally anticipated. In our view this is partly because of the financial strait-jacket within which local authorities have had to operate. The recent climate has actually discouraged innovation and managed change, which tend to require higher rather than lower spending in the short term.

Even so major cultural changes are under way which, in some authorities, have already led to the introduction of different organisational structures. Financial management functions have been a key part of this process and many local authority finance staff have now experienced externalisation or decentralisation. The culture which has now emerged focuses on:

- **competition** – this has now permeated almost every area of financial management;

- **cost reduction** – particularly in relation to overhead costs;

- **purchaser/provider split** – a much sharper and more business-like relationship between support service providers and their customers.

We believe that local authorities are now approaching a crossroads. A more sympathetic climate may emerge fairly soon for local government as a whole, although we can see no return to the 'good old days'! If opportunities to refocus on local needs and aspirations do arise, it will be important for these opportunities to be grasped firmly. The skills and experience which have been acquired so painfully during the first half of the 1990s should then stand us in good stead. As long as there are sufficient reserves of energy to match the considerable expertise and commitment around us, we believe that local government is well placed to play a full part in the partnership which hopefully will take this country into the twenty-first century.

1

Financial management in context

KEY POINTS

- Financial management is one element of the overall management matrix.

- The task of management is to achieve the organisation's objectives as effectively, economically and efficiently as possible.

- Financial management covers a wide range of functions, not all of which are carried out wholly in the CFO's department.

- A highly centralised approach to financial management is unlikely to promote maximum effectiveness in service delivery.

- In principle the process of financial management decentralisation should only be constrained by valid considerations of efficiency and accountability.

- In practice local authorities have responded in a variety of ways to the legislative and resource pressures of the first half of the 1990s.

- The extent to which decentralisation of financial management functions is possible in the future will also depend on resource issues and political considerations, both national and local.

Financial management functions

Management is about getting things done! A more rigorous definition is that management is concerned with the acquisition, development and utilisation of resources to achieve certain goals.

Purists might well argue that this definition is only partial because management also encompasses the process of establishing goals and, of course, reviewing performance. This criticism is fair but the above partial definition nevertheless has merit, particularly in the local government context, where establishing goals is not purely a management prerogative.

Financial management concentrates on the resource of money. This is not to deny the importance of the other resources, namely:

- human resources;

- physical resources;

- information and knowledge.

Indeed, money derives its significance largely because it is usually needed to acquire the other 'productive' resources.

This description should at least make it clear that, for the most part, financial management is not an end in itself. It is a means to an end. It is one part of the management matrix which should be helping to achieve the organisation's goals as effectively, efficiently and economically as possible. This applies to all organisations, whether in the public or the private sector.

That's all very well but what is financial management really about – what functions does it encompass? Before referring to the checklist at Appendix A, you should attempt to compile your own list. The first item might well be the payment of salaries and wages; we mention this in case you are finding it difficult to think of any useful financial management functions!

When you come to compare your list with Appendix A, you may find that a number of the items listed in the Appendix are missing from your own list. There could be various reasons for this but two, in particular, need to be emphasised at this point, namely:

- lack of basic awareness of financial functions;

- confusion between financial management and the functions carried out by the CFO's staff.

If the first of these reasons applies and you were indeed unaware of several of the functions listed in Appendix A, particularly those in categories 1 and 2, then we refer you to Chapters 6–8, where you will find a description of the purposes and basic procedures associated with each function.

Another possibility, however, is that you have listed most or all of the functions currently performed by the CFO's department in your authority. If so, you may have omitted any financial management functions which are carried out wholly or partly in other departments or indeed other organisations. For example housing rent collection may well be the responsibility of your Director of Housing, rather than you CFO. If you work in a District or Borough Council your superannuation may be dealt with by a nearby District Council (in metropolitan areas) or by the County Council.

There is a further possibility, namely that certain functions, particularly some of those in category 3, do not yet play a significant part in the management scheme of your authority. You will almost certainly have come across the concept of value for money but quite possibly in the shape of *ad hoc* corporate initiatives rather than as a routine management function. It is probably fair to say that categories 1 and 2 of Appendix A represent those financial management functions which have traditionally been the prerogative of the CFO and his or her staff and are carried out by all local authorities.

Traditionally there has been a highly centralised structure across local authorities for these aspects of financial management, with the CFO being directly responsible for most or all functions throughout the entire Council. He or she has also been the line manager of the vast majority of specialist finance staff, and these staff have been organised within the CFO's department in functional teams e.g. payroll, internal audit, rather than in service-based teams e.g. education, housing. The main arguments in support of this approach have been those of economy and efficiency.

One of the key issues raised in this book is the merit of decentralising some of these functions to bring them as near as possible to the point of service delivery. This is a vital issue for local authority financial management because:

- there is a growing awareness that a highly centralised approach does not always help to achieve the most effective delivery of services to the community;

- statutory developments, such as LMS and CCT require a more decentralised approach;

- developments in IT and communications have made possible major improvements in the quantity and quality of financial management information and training which can be made available to all managers.

It is considered that a decentralised approach to traditional areas of financial management does help to maximise the relevance and responsiveness of the services for which local government is responsible. Ideally, the extent of this process should only be limited by valid considerations of efficiency and accountability. This issue will be covered in more detail in Chapter 3.

The functions in category 3 of Appendix A tend to reflect some of the more recent challenges facing local authority financial management. They have developed in importance during the first half of the 1990s and will be commonplace by the millennium. It is very unlikely that any of these newer functions, with the possible exception of investment management, is or will be the sole preserve of the CFO's staff.

A word about information advice in category 3; it may appear spurious to include the provision of management information as a financial management function but effective management can only take place on the basis of adequate management information. Information must be accurate, timely, relevant and intelligible; the last criterion is becoming increasingly important as decentralisation of decision-making proceeds. The crucial role of training in supporting a decentralised framework of financial management cannot be overemphasised. In recent years there have often been only limited benefits from new management structures and operating procedures because insufficient attention has been paid to training needs, and the resources required to satisfy them. We shall reiterate this message in later chapters.

Performance standards and charters have become highly topical in local government in recent years and seem likely to remain so. It is in the area of performance review that a clear distinction can be made in financial management terms between the public and private sectors. In the private sector money is widely used to measure the success of an organisation. Goals and results are usually expressed in cash terms with respect to profit, output, sales, dividends or return on capital employed. These criteria are either unavailable or irrelevant in many parts of the public sector. In the past this has meant that there has been a tendency in the public sector to concentrate on resource inputs which can be converted into the common denominator of money, rather than on output or effectiveness. The Chartered Institute of Public Finance and Accountancy (CIPFA), the Audit Commission and others have striven for many years to develop techniques for performance measurement in local government. During the 1990s there has been strong encouragement from central government for this work. For example, comparative performance indicators for local authorities are now an annual event. In our view, however, the impact of charters and performance indicators has, up to now, been limited and, in some cases, perverse. The reasons for this are explored further in Chapters 3, 8 and 10.

Achieving effective financial management

Effective management can never be guaranteed because it involves decision-making by human beings. However, there are certain conditions which will encourage effective management within an organisation and they are as important for financial management as for any other sphere of management. They are relevant whatever management structure is in place and include:

- the existence of clear objectives at all levels of management;

- well-defined levels of authority and responsibility throughout the management structure;

- easy access to accurate, up-to-date and understandable management information;

- sensible and straightforward control and reporting procedures;

- access to proper training and advice;

- the employment of effective systems for monitoring performance.

These requirements apply whether all the financial management functions listed in Appendix A are carried out by a central finance department or not. However, it is fairly easy to see that, where certain financial management functions are decentralised and particularly where responsibilities are shared between service departments and the CFO's department, these criteria will be even more crucial and yet at the same time more difficult to achieve. For example, many authorities possess financial information systems which are satisfactory where the user has financial expertise, but are unsuitable for non-finance users. Such systems are proving more and more problematic as the demands on local authority managers increase, particularly if financial management is decentralised.

Within local government the situation is further complicated by the spread of financial decision-making across at least three levels, namely:

- the individual establishment, unit or team;

- the service department or committee; and

- the CFO's department.

Decision-makers at each of these levels will have differing perspectives, needs and priorities. In terms of objectives, the establishment manager and, to a lesser extent, the service department manager may well be more concerned about effective service delivery than about the economic and efficient use of resources. Information needs will clearly differ in terms of both the level of detail and the format and content of reports. The establishment manager will want maximum flexibility and therefore limited financial controls, whereas the service department manager and the financial manager in the CFO's department may place greater emphasis on adequate controls over such measures as budget transfers (virement) and carry forwards. Training needs will clearly differ. These issues are considered in Chapter 3.

The above differences have been brought into even sharper focus by the progressive exposure of local authority services to CCT. There is now a wide range of services for which local authorities are required to test their in-house operations in the market place, and to apply private sector measures of financial performance such as return on capital employed. This has necessitated a fundamental redesign of objectives, responsibilities and controls and a thorough review of information and training needs. Chapter 4 will focus on these challenges.

Rapid change should, at first sight, provide the sort of dynamic environment in which improved models of financial management emerge naturally. In practice, it appears that CFOs have been preoccupied with so many statutory changes during the first half of the 1990s that there has been less impetus from above to decentralise financial management functions than we would initially have expected. In addition, the ever tighter squeeze on local authority finance, as well as being an added distraction for CFOs, has placed a premium on reducing costs, rather than making more effective use of existing resources. As LMS has demonstrated, decentralised management may well be more effective, but it is not cheaper, at least in the short term.

In the face of such major pressures it is important to stress that there is no question of any of the financial management functions in Appendix A becoming obsolete or unnecessary. Indeed, the role of financial management is very much intact. What has been changing to some extent in recent years is the approach to financial management, and especially the structural and procedural framework within which it is exercised. There are now a variety of structures within local government, both for managing the delivery of services and for supporting this process. It remains to be seen whether, by the end of the 1990s, the present diversity will have increased, or whether a degree of uniformity will emerge in the light of local and national political pressures and, to a lesser extent, successes and failures in the meantime.

2

The chief financial officer's role

KEY POINTS

- The CFO has a wide-ranging statutory responsibility to ensure financial integrity (probity).

- Initiatives to decentralise financial management, whether imposed by legislation or not, must avoid any material loss of probity.

- Subject to this the CFO can relinquish direct control of many financial management functions as long as effective monitoring and reporting procedures are in place.

- Certain core functions are best retained centrally under the direct control of the CFO.

- These functions relate to the co-ordination of budgeting, final accounts and certain internal audit work, financial training and technical tasks, such as insurance.

Introduction

The role of the CFO is a key element in any debate about financial management in local government. Before embarking on this debate it is essential to appreciate the environment in which the CFO operates and to recognise that there are well-defined statutory powers and legal precedents, which give the CFO clear and very wide responsibilities in relation to the financial affairs of the local authority. This is sometimes a bone of contention with both councillors and service departments and it is important that all concerned are aware of the well-established framework which is the

7

starting-point for any changes to existing financial structures and procedures.

Local authorities, as public bodies responsible for services to the community, must be able to account for all their actions. Obviously the fact that ultimate authority rests with elected councillors provides the main vehicle for ensuring political accountability, but other mechanisms are required to achieve professional and managerial accountability.

As their title suggests, accountants are employed to account for the financial transactions of organisations, and local authority accountants are no exception. In this narrow, traditional sense, accounting seems to be a process which takes place after the event in order to validate, in some way, what took place. The fact that many of our colleagues now prefer to be called financial managers properly reflects the fact that their role is now much wider and more proactive than the title 'accountant' implies. However, in our view it is still perfectly fair to say that a primary task of all local authority finance managers, and especially the CFO, is to secure financial accountability.

This principle has recently been reinforced by the Nolan Committee on standards in public life, in its second report covering local public spending bodies. Strictly speaking, local authorities are outside the scope of the report, which focuses on unelected independent bodies such as training and enterprise councils (TECs) and grant maintained schools. Even so the central recommendation should strike a chord with local government managers. This is that 'central control . . . should be limited as far as possible to setting policy guidelines and operating boundaries, to ensuring an effective audit framework, and to the effective deployment of sanctions'.

It is useful to explore financial accountability in the context of the earlier, albeit crude definition of financial management which talked of 'achieving the organisation's goals as effectively, efficiently and economically as possible'. On this basis it could be argued that accountability is achieved if it can be demonstrated that the stated objectives have been achieved (effectiveness) in an orderly and timely manner (efficiency) at reasonable cost and without waste (economy). It is therefore necessary for the CFO to ensure that financial procedures, controls and information are in place to satisfy these requirements.

It is not hard to see that financial accountability in local government must go some way beyond this to encompass financial integrity (probity). Not only must the financial affairs of a local authority be managed prudently (economy), they must also be free from fraud or corruption.

Understandably CFOs, in seeking to guard the status and authority of their role, are keen to emphasise that the strong tradition of financial integrity in local government is largely due to the way they have tackled their duties. Despite occasional, well-publicised cases of fraud and corruption in local councils, few people would claim that financial processes in local government are inherently unsatisfactory in terms of probity. Indeed, it is probably safe to argue that neither the elected member, nor the public generally, would want to see the financial probity of local government undermined.

However, critics of the CFO's traditional role could argue with some justification that there has previously been too much emphasis by CFOs on economy and probity and not enough on effectiveness and efficiency, i.e. on ensuring that service objectives are met in a way which secures good value for money. In addition, more and more attention has been paid in recent years to another aspect of accountability, which may be described as 'transparency'. This is achieved where accurate, relevant and timely information is provided which the user can understand.

A lot of effort has already gone into making published financial information about local authorities and other public bodies more intelligible, much of it under the auspices of CIPFA. There are now codes of practice covering various aspects of financial reporting which, although voluntary, provide the standards against which financial statements are audited and, in some cases, are endorsed by Government.

Of course, published financial information is only the tip of the iceberg and it is equally important for service managers in local authorities to see an improvement in the transparency of the financial management which they receive. The overall aim in reviewing traditional approaches to financial management must therefore be to improve effectiveness, value for money and transparency without any material loss of probity.

Statutory responsibilities

There are three main elements to the statutory responsibilities of a CFO. These can be summarised briefly as follows:

- **The case of *Attorney General v De Winton* in 1906**   This case established that the CFO has a direct fiduciary relationship with ratepayers. He cannot plead that he is acting under the instruction of the Council as an excuse for an illegal act. Subsequently, the 'Wednesbury Case' developed this principle by providing for a local authority's actions to be challenged in the courts on the grounds of unreasonableness as well as illegality. Clearly this places an added onus on the CFO who effectively has to provide the ultimate authorisation for any expenditure by signing the cheque.

- **Section 151 of the Local Government Act 1972**   Section 151 imposes a clear statutory responsibility on the CFO. It requires that 'every local authority shall make arrangements for the proper administration of their financial affairs and shall secure that one of their officers has responsibility for the administration of those affairs'. An immediate consequence of this statute was that more prominence was given to internal audit. Financial regulations, which are the formal means of giving effect to these statutory duties within a local authority, were generally revised at this time and have since remained unchanged in many authorities until quite recently.

- **Section 114 of the Local Government Finance Act 1988**   There is now a duty on every CFO to report directly to elected members if he or she believes an illegal act might take place or if expenditure might exceed available resources. This places the CFO in a potentially delicate and exposed position given that he or she may have to challenge the intentions of his or her employer. This has become known as the 'whistle-blowing' role of the CFO but its impact to date is far from clear.

It is important to understand that this statutory framework places the local authority CFO in a more authoritative, but also more exposed, position than that of a finance director in a private or public company. When specific statutory responsibilities rest on a particular individual, that person neglects them at his or her peril! The CFO must therefore ensure, at the very least, that arrangements are in place to cover these responsibilities. Such arrangements may take various forms, ranging from dedicated finance staff to written manuals setting out financial procedures, regulations and minimum standards. Inevitably, they increase the cost and complexity of transacting local authority business. This is a legitimate reason why councils' overhead costs may be higher than those in the private sector and also why, in some cases, procedures are required which appear cumbersome and onerous to service managers, councillors and the general public.

By way of a footnote to this section, it should be pointed out that the CFO's statutory responsibility for internal audit as the 'responsible financial officer' under the 1972 Act may soon be removed. The Government intends to amend the Accounts and Audit Regulations to transfer ultimate responsibility for effective internal audit to the Council as a whole. The thinking seems to be that this will enable the internal audit function to establish reporting lines which are independent of the financial management function, and are therefore more effective in protecting the wider interests of the Authority. Not surprisingly, this proposal is being opposed by CIPFA on behalf of CFOs, most of whom are its members.

The scope of a CFO's responsibilities

The wording of the 1972 Act is sufficiently comprehensive to encompass all financial transactions that take place in a local authority. The CFO's responsibilities therefore cover a major proportion of a local authority's operations. Given this wide span of control, there has to be some trade-off between probity and efficiency; otherwise arrangements could become so riddled with time-consuming and costly checks that they would become inefficient to operate. It is one of the tasks of the CFO to determine for each area of the Council's operations the extent and nature of these trade-offs. Risk analysis, particularly in relation to the audit function, is therefore an increasingly common feature of financial management procedures. This technique is covered in more detail in Chapter 8.

A major point that non-finance managers increasingly recognise, however, is that, although the CFO carries the responsibility for effective financial control, he or she need not use his or her own staff to undertake this work. Chief financial officers have widely differing views on this. One only has to observe the varying degrees to which the finance function has already been decentralised, and the variety of methods used, to realise that there is no consensus on this issue. This topic recurs frequently in the pages that follow.

The range of financial management functions which are likely to be carried out in a local authority is listed in Appendix A and described in more detail in Chapters 6–8. Some of these functions, particularly those in categories 1 and 2 of Appendix A, flow directly from the CFO's statutory responsibilities. They must therefore either be under the direct control of the CFO or be carried out in accordance with his or her requirements.

Core functions

The remainder of this chapter is a description of what we feel should be the core finance functions in a regime where there is maximum decentralisation of financial management. They represent the financial management functions which the CFO should always carry out directly, rather than decentralise or delegate to another department or agency. The core functions defined below go beyond the costs of 'service strategy and regulation' as defined by CIPFA in its 'Statement on Accounting for Overheads in Local Authorities' which is now a subsidiary part of the Code of Practice on Local Authority Accounting. This is relevant because the Statement only allows those support service costs, including financial management, which relate to service strategy and regulation to be reported separately; all other financial management costs must be spread across service departments, trading activities, other departments and other agencies, preferably as charges based on actual usage. A proportion, at least, of the costs of the core functions described below would therefore have to be allocated or apportioned to service departments.

Accounting for overheads is an important aspect of transparency and accountability, because its purpose is to make clear the full cost of local authorities' 'front line' services. It is also vital in pursuing initiatives which promote competition, e.g. CCT, or delegation, e.g. LMS. However, as we can see here, there is not always complete identity between the quest for accountability and the need for probity.

In general, we believe that the CFO can fulfil his or her responsibilities by setting clear minimum standards for all financial management functions. Alongside these standards the CFO must create monitoring and reporting procedures to confirm that all parts of the organisation are functioning safely and efficiently in financial management terms, or to enable timely corrective action to be taken if this is not the case. This should become the CFO's prime focus and would then make it possible for much of the routine financial work which the CFO's staff have traditionally performed to be organised in other ways. Within this framework there are two types of financial management function over which the CFO is likely to retain direct control:

- **Co-ordination** There is an important co-ordinating role associated with preparing a Council's overall capital and revenue budgets and final accounts. This annual task will always have to be centralised, even if the vast majority of detailed work is done outside the CFO's department. There will also be a need for a corporate financial input into the strategic planning process, if the authority has one.

- **Technical** Functions of a corporate or technical nature, such as Council tax collection, VAT, insurance, cash flow and borrowing, are best retained within the core. First, there are unlikely to be sufficient skills in other departments to carry out such specialised work effectively and secondly there are economies of scale to be gained by central provision. A similar argument can be made for superannuation administration, where expertise is already concentrated in one tier of local authority.

The above approach envisages a large proportion of financial management functions being undertaken either via business units within the CFO's department or outside the CFO's department altogether. This could encompass most elements of the payroll, creditor payments, housing benefits, income, financial planning, budgetary control and final accounts functions, as well as any statutory returns and grant claims which relate to a single service.

Internal audit

There has been no reference to internal audit in the scenario outlined above. The commentary in Chapter 8 makes clear that internal audit must be *independent* and that it should provide a *service to all levels of management*. The former requirement suggests that basing internal audit staff within service departments may not be appropriate. The latter requirement can only be achieved in practice, however, if the internal auditor has a sound knowledge of and a degree of rapport with the service which he or she is auditing. Consequently, we believe that some aspects of internal audit work could be undertaken quite satisfactorily by staff based within a service department, particularly for large-scale and complex services such as education, social services and housing.

This is a practical example of the trade-off between probity and efficiency. Provided the auditor does not have a conflict of interest and there are reasonable checks built into the system, there is no reason why some service activities should not be audited by a member of the same service department. The CFO should establish at the outset that all audit personnel in the service department can give objective and unfettered advice to service management and, if the occasion merits it, have direct access to the CFO. This is no different in principle from the internal auditor in the CFO's department having direct access to the Chief Executive or Chairman of the Finance Committee, when he or she wishes to question the CFO's actions.

This is one of several areas of financial management where experienced finance staff, who are becoming increasingly scarce, can specialise in specific service areas and work closely with the service managers in those areas. Many large private companies are organised in this way. It can be argued that, subject to proper safeguards as set out above, such an approach is likely to achieve better value for money than the traditional centralised arrangements.

There are sound practical reasons why internal audit cannot be decentralised fully to service departments. For example, there is a requirement for a planned audit programme to be drawn up. It is not appropriate for this to be done by service managers on their own although it should be done in conjunction with them. Once in place, this programme would probably have to be undertaken by two sets of people. The basic audit work could be done by the CFO's staff or appropriately trained staff in the service department. The more complicated and higher-risk work, certainly that involving computer systems and processes, would need to be done by specialist staff from the CFO's department. These staff would in fact have four functions:

- to co-ordinate and monitor the service departments' annual audit programme;

- to carry out some of the audit work themselves, particularly in relation to computer processes and the associated controls;

- to set overall audit standards, train personnel and monitor the quality of audit work carried out;

- to liaise closely with the external auditors.

This central audit team should be experienced, qualified and highly trained, but small in number. One of its major functions would be to monitor national developments in audit standards and to provide relevant training and advice to staff throughout the authority.

A partially decentralised system of internal audit would need to incorporate severe sanctions against any auditor within a service department who was found to be shirking the difficult responsibility of giving totally objective and impartial advice. It is important for everyone to understand these possible difficulties. They are not dissimilar to the difficulties CFOs themselves may have to face in relation to the Section 114 duties in the Local Government Finance Act 1988.

Budget and accounts preparation

Relationships on the side of accountancy and budget preparation are likely to be more straightforward. For these functions, the CFO would retain a small, highly qualified core team to:

- review and advise on the corporate financial strategy;

- prepare the local authority revenue budget each year and calculate, where necessary, the resources needed to finance it;

- prepare the local authority capital budget and advise on how this should be funded;

- monitor both budgets, in overall terms, during the course of the year;

- prepare the final accounts and see them through the external audit process;

- prepare those returns and statistics which can only be done centrally.

In order to be able to co-ordinate this work and produce accurate consolidated financial statements, it is important that this team of people should set clear accounting standards and guidelines for all departments to follow. There must be a very clear central direction of the consolidation process, whether the exercise is budget preparation, budget monitoring or closure of accounts. However, it should not be necessary for the CFO's staff to dictate or standardise the financial information used by service managers, although there is advantage in making the interface between the CFO's requirements and those of the service manager as simple as possible.

The other major role for the central accountancy team would, as for the central audit team, be one of training. It would be expected to keep up with best practice and hold regular training seminars with the relevant finance staff in service departments. Many organisations already use chief or development accountants to perform this function in relation to finance department staff.

Exchequer functions

The major financial decentralisation battleground is exchequer, which covers the functions of payroll, creditors and income. Developments in IT are progressively making redundant the physical movement of pieces of paper, like timesheets and invoices, between establishments or offices. Direct input by establishments makes the processes potentially much more efficient. However, the risk factor also increases; hence there needs to be enhanced internal control and audit to safeguard probity.

The CFO needs to be satisfied that:

(a) the central internal audit team has sufficient resources and expertise to ensure that the exchequer computer systems are secure;

(b) there are controls within the exchequer functions which will enable corporate objectives to be met; and

(c) new developments, either locally or nationally, are capable of effective implementation.

We have already dealt with item (a) above. As for (b), there is a need to retain the kind of role that payroll and payments sections managers have traditionally performed, such as co-ordinating the implementation of national pay awards. In addition most organisations have performance standards such as:

- paying 95 per cent of all invoices received within six weeks;

- income arrears should be within 5 per cent of the gross debit within two months of despatch of the bill;

- complaints should not exceed 0.1 per cent of the number of transactions.

This kind of information has to be collected, analysed and monitored. A central resource is therefore required.

To the extent that there are still corporate IT systems to deal with payment of accounts and payroll, system enhancements and changes will affect all departments. It will be a core function to advise on developments and on priority for implementation, after proper consultation with users.

Finally, any central exchequer resource should:

- set and monitor exchequer standards;

- play a lead role in the training and development of exchequer personnel;

- co-ordinate any exchequer changes required by legislation or national developments, e.g. national pay awards, changes in national insurance regulations.

There must be a close relationship between the CFO's internal audit team and these other core personnel, particularly in relation to the development of corporate financial systems.

The CFO's core functions are now complete. In our view they comprise:

- an audit co-ordination, control and training team;

- a budget and accountancy co-ordination, control and training team;

- an exchequer co-ordination, control, training and systems development team;

- specialist functions which might include:

  - superannuation;

  - council tax collection;

  - VAT administration;

  - insurance;

  - cash flow management;

  - debt management;

  - investment management.

Organisational changes along these lines have taken place over the last five years, although it would be misleading to suggest that a uniform pattern or pace of development has emerged. Other chapters in this book will examine the potential implications of decentralising all but the CFO's core finance functions for service managers and for others at the heart of local authority decision-making.

3

Decentralising financial management

KEY POINTS

- The recent emphasis on decentralisation of decision-making provides the opportunity for total management at the point of service delivery.

- In order for decentralised financial management to be effective:

  - Traditional financial control and reporting procedures must be streamlined and made more flexible.

  - Objectives and responsibilities must be clearly defined.

  - Financial information for local managers may have to be adapted and improved.

  - Considerable financial training and guidance must be provided to local managers.

- Decentralisation is unlikely to be appropriate or successful if it is introduced to reduce costs in the short term.

- A corporate approach to decentralisation is essential.

Introduction

Recent legislation on CCT and LMS has placed statutory pressure on local government to embrace decentralisation of decision-making. The problems posed by this process of change have been aired briefly in Chapter 2. In this chapter we aim to explore in more detail the opportunities and risks which face managers in those local authority establishments and service departments where efforts are made to decentralise, particularly where financial management is part of this process.

Broadly speaking the opportunity is for these managers to have effective control over all the resources they employ – personnel, property, money and information – and hence the ability to exercise total management. The risk is that total management at or near the point of service delivery will be inefficient, uneconomic and ultimately ineffective. This will occur if:

- existing control and reporting procedures are not adjusted to meet the new requirements; and/or

- local managers base their decisions on inadequate awareness, expertise and management information.

The discussion in this chapter is based on a typical local authority scenario in which a service department supports a number of outside establishments. Although the establishments will probably be the main service providers, it is quite possible that the service departments will also have some responsibilities for direct service provision. The education service within a county council or metropolitan district council is a good example. Schools and other outside education establishments will be the main service providers, but some important services, such as student awards and school transport administration, are likely to be delivered from the centre. In the remainder of this chapter we shall use the term 'managers' to cover all those who have direct responsibility for service provision, whether based centrally within service departments or in outside establishments. We shall also refer to 'budget holders'; these are, or should be, individual managers who have the responsibility both for managing a particular service activity and for controlling expenditure on that activity against the amounts provided in the annual revenue budget. Budget holders can operate either in service departments or in outside establishments but it is essential that there is one and only one budget holder for each part of the budget and that there are clear guidelines for determining responsibilities.

The direct impact of recent legislation is confined to a fairly narrow range of financial management functions. For example, LMS delegates responsibility for major aspects of financial planning and budgetary control from the centre to individual governing bodies and heads. There is no specific requirement at present for local education authorities (LEAs) to transfer any other financial management functions to LMS schools, although information regarding the costs of financial and other support services should be made available to schools.

The purpose of these comments is not to play down the significance of LMS;

indeed it has had a profound impact on local government over the last five or six years. However, it is important to remember that many important financial management functions, such as payroll, creditor payments and internal audit, have not yet been directly affected by the statutory decentralisation initiatives. What the legislation on CCT and LMS is certainly bringing to the fore is interest in the effectiveness and efficiency with which all financial management functions are carried out, and of course their cost.

Current problems

At present, management decisions in local authorities are subject to various constraints. Some of these constraints are formal and explicit and relate primarily to financial management issues. These include:

- **Policy**   Managers are subject to the policy decisions of elected members and to financial plans, usually in the form of capital and annual revenue budgets, which are approved in order to implement those decisions. In addition there are various procedural constraints whose main purpose is to limit the ability of managers to depart from the approved policies. A good example is the treatment of virement. In most local authorities there are strict rules which must be followed if a manager wishes to use money voted for one part of the budget, e.g. equipment, to spend in another part of the budget, e.g. staff.

- **Probity**   Alongside and often interlinking with the policy constraints are the formal rules which are usually set out in financial regulations and which enable the CFO to fulfil the statutory responsibilities described in the previous chapter. These regulations may cover such diverse activities as handling petty cash and authorising a major capital project. This will be discussed in more detail in the next chapter.

There is no doubt that the administrative structures and processes which have been established to cope with these characteristics of local government, namely the authority of elected members and the need for probity, have rendered local authority decision-making complicated and often time consuming, especially by comparison with some parts of the private sector. Even before the advent of recent legislation, many were beginning to question whether the entire paraphernalia of controls embodied in standing orders and financial regulations were necessary as they stood to safeguard the authority of members and the peace of mind of the CFO. More significantly perhaps there was an increasing recognition that certain controls should be loosened in order to achieve a better balance between probity and effectiveness.

The opportunities

In financial management terms what recent legislation has sought to do is to oblige local authorities to concentrate on:

- establishing service objectives in output terms for the areas affected;

- providing sufficient overall cash resources to enable these objectives to be achieved economically and efficiently; and

- monitoring the extent to which the objectives are in fact achieved.

This is far removed from the detailed and rigid controls, invariably expressed in terms of resource inputs, which are embodied in the traditional annual revenue budget and the financial regulations that govern budget holders. In many local authorities it is still the case that the majority of budget holders not merely are constrained to a spending total, but also face separate and specific limits on what they can spend in each area of their budget – professional staff, support staff, premises, costs, transport costs, supplies and services and so on. Indeed in certain key areas such as staffing there may well be total control by the centre so that the budget holder has little or no discretion regarding recruitment, levels of pay or service conditions.

In direct service organisations (DSOs) and LMS schools these detailed controls can no longer be applied. As well as having clear information about the total resources available to them, managers have considerable flexibility as to how those resources are applied. Virements and carry forwards from one financial year to the next are possible without reference to the centre. Establishments are no longer obliged to obtain goods and services from suppliers nominated by the Council. At the formal level, therefore, total management at the point of service delivery will become a practical possibility rather than a distant ideal.

At first sight, decentralisation appears to be good news for the managers concerned. Admittedly, it is possible to spot one or two drawbacks. For example, it is certainly true that automatic central funding in full of pay awards and general inflation will not necessarily apply to delegated budgets, even if it did before, and this could cause some local discomfort. However, the major loser from decentralisation seems to be the CFO whose statutory responsibilities with regard to these activities remain but who has lost many of the direct controls previously deemed essential to fulfil them. In our view the best strategy for the CFO under these circumstances is to define and monitor sensible minimum standards and also to ensure that managers are provided with appropriate training, guidance and information so that their financial management is both imaginative and sound.

The risks

In most local authorities the formal constraints under which managers currently operate are compounded by variety of other obstacles. These include:

- the absence of clear objectives;

- blurred responsibilities and accountabilities;

- a shortage of useful and timely management information;

- even more restrictive and cumbersome control and reporting procedures than are legitimately required for reasons of policy and probity;

- inadequate access to training and advice;

- a total absence of performance review;

- restricted access to transitional or development funds.

Each of these is a serious barrier to effective management. Together they represent an environment in which existing management performance is likely to be unsatisfactory, but where attempts to decentralise decision-making would be futile even if they have statutory backing.

The need for clear objectives is now so well recognised that little further comment ought to be needed. However, formalising and communicating objectives is a difficult and time-consuming exercise in a large organisation because there needs to be a hierarchy of compatible and consistent objectives to overlay the organisation's management structure. Each manager should understand clearly what he or she is expected to achieve and how this will contribute to achieving the overall objectives of the organisation. Initial forays into this area can easily become bogged down and then take second place to more urgent management commitments. Our advice would be to persevere to the end but not to aim for perfection first time round; there will be ample opportunity for refinement when objectives are reviewed, as they must be periodically.

Service managers in local government do not in general have neat, well-defined spheres of operation. Overlapping responsibilities and strong interdependencies abound in most service departments. In addition, there may be managers within service departments, and even a few within larger establishments, who are not directly involved in service provision but who exercise some sort of co-ordinating, advisory or supervisory role. Under these circumstances it is very easy for financial management responsibilities to become blurred. If this occurs effective financial management will be much more difficult to achieve, particularly in certain key control areas such as budgeting and budgetary control.

Given the high incidence of centralised mainframe financial systems in local government, it is likely that most centrally located local authority managers will have access to a plentiful supply of financial information. Whether this information is relevant, up to date or easy to understand is another matter. Managers in outside establishments may be even less fortunate. This topic will be covered more fully in Chapter 5.

In all organisations systems and procedures are governed not only by current requirements but also by precedent and tradition. The temptation to stick with familiar methods can never be underestimated. Even where there is willingness to move with the times, the increasing pace of change in local government can make it difficult in practice to do so. If financial control procedures are to remain credible, they must continually be reviewed and adapted in the light of statutory changes, new demands on services and improvements in IT. Otherwise they will eventually become discredited in the eyes of non-finance managers, and will then be evaded or totally ignored.

If certain financial management functions and decisions are to be decentralised successfully to staff who are not financially qualified and have little or no previous experience of financial management, some training is obviously necessary. The introduction of LMS provides a very clear illustration of the considerable training burden which is created by the need to spread financial awareness and expertise across a numerically large, varied and widely dispersed group. Although such a commitment is almost certainly beyond the immediate resources of the CFO and his or her staff, the fact remains that a much greater proportion of the CFO's resources should now be devoted to training than has been the case in the past.

The point has already been made that, in financial terms, reviewing performance is much more straightforward in the private sector than in the public sector. Nevertheless the nettle of performance review has to be grasped; otherwise the entire process may lose direction and purpose. As with objective setting we would recommend a pragmatic approach which builds over time on the possibly small number of performance indicators which are both relevant and, at least at the outset, capable of being measured. Information technology has an important part to play in the development of performance indicators. The increasing capability of IT systems to capture, store, analyse and present both financial and non-financial data is almost certainly the key to ultimate success. However, there is still a long way to go for most of us!

For some time, local authority managers have been under a continuous imperative to reduce costs. The CFO and his/her staff are certainly not exempt from this pressure, and are usually expected to be at the forefront of cost-cutting initiatives. It is probably safe to suggest that, in general, decentralisation initiatives do not generate cost savings in the short term. Indeed, given the additional training and information needs that are generated, they may increase costs for a transitional period. This gives rise to two possibilities, both of which we have experienced in practice. The first is that decentralisation is rejected in favour of an alternative approach which does offer the prospect of immediate cost savings, such as contracting out. The second is that decentralisation takes place but is later abandoned or curtailed; this is very likely if unrealistic projections have been made about future cost savings, in terms of both scale and timing. Rather than being a stimulus to management innovation, the requirement to cut costs in the short term is likely to be a barrier to many worthwhile developments.

Some solutions

The above commentary raises a formidable catalogue of problems, some of which fellow practitioners will recognise from their own experience. However, their existence should not be used as an excuse for inaction; indeed such problems should be tackled as a matter of urgency whether or not decentralisation is on the agenda. The key message is that successful decentralisation will almost certainly require a great deal of preparatory work to achieve:

- an agreed corporate strategy which is reflected in the business plan for the CFO's department and the other departments affected;

- a clear corporate framework of management responsibilities and support service relationships to underpin the proposed changes (*see* Chapter 9 and Appendix D);

- revised standing orders and financial regulations to reflect the realities of the new arrangements (*see* Chapter 4);

- improved management information systems (and particularly the financial information systems) within the organisation and a flexible corporate strategy for their future development (*see* Chapter 5);

- regular formal staff review and development for all staff involved;

- a co-ordinated and properly resourced training programme for these staff, with particular emphasis on financial management;

- a clear service focus within the CFO's department and a high level of commitment to the new arrangements;

- a multi-disciplinary project approach to implementation and to dealing with unforeseen problems and new requirements.

This may seem a daunting list but many local authorities have already adopted some of these measures and there may be some authorities that have done all this and much more. It may be intriguing to some readers that we envisage a corporate approach. What is increasingly clear to us is that success in decentralising decision-making in local authorities requires both a major corporate commitment and the retention of an influential, if not numerically strong, central core.

4

Compulsory competitive tendering

- CCT continues to pose a major challenge to finance personnel and systems.

- The business culture associated with CCT has already been felt by those financial managers providing support services to DSOs.

- The impact of extending CCT to white-collar services, including finance, is not yet clear.

- The need to split the client and contractor responsibilities has required a reorganisation of traditional structures and relationships in those service areas subject to CCT.

- The competitive pressures which DSOs face mean that they must have access to:

  - efficient exchequer services;

  - expert advice on business planning and forecasting;

  - relevant and timely costing information; and

  - adequate technical support;

  at a competitive price.

- DSOs cannot operate under the tight financial regulations which have traditionally applied to local authority services.

- The statutory framework for CCT is still in a state of flux.

Introduction

Compulsory competitive tendering applies to a growing range of local authority services. The basic principle of CCT is that, if an authority wishes to deliver a specified service using its own work-force, it must first put the work out to tender and consider private sector bids to provide the service alongside the bid of its own work-force. There is an expectation that the tender which imposes least cost on the local authority will be successful, and that the local authority will not subsidise an in-house tender to undercut competition from outside. To achieve these aims, the Government has generated a complex web of statutory regulations.

It is sometimes difficult to appreciate that CCT has been part of the local authority scene since 1980. The Local Government Planning and Land Act 1980 brought competition into the areas of housing repairs, highway maintenance and sewerage agency work. Direct labour organisations (DLOs) were established in most local authorities to compete for work which had previously been theirs by right. The majority of those DLOs are still in business today. Under the 1988 Local Government Act, which enables any local authority service to be brought within the competition net, CCT was first extended to:

- schools and welfare catering;

- refuse collection;

- vehicle maintenance;

- grounds maintenance;

- street cleaning;

- cleaning of buildings;

- management of sports and leisure facilities.

Once these services were operating within the CCT framework, the Government switched its attention to 'white-collar' services. Over the last four years there have been lengthy preparations to bring legal services, IT, finance, personnel, housing management and construction related services (engineering, architecture and property management) within the CCT umbrella. Compulsory competition has also been extended to cover waste disposal under legislation which requires local authorities to set up internal waste disposal companies in order to compete for work. Social services have not escaped from the drive for competition, with both residential and community care now being subject to requirements and targets which impose a market-based approach.

27

After 15 years of grappling with CCT, at no little cost in terms of time and energy, the position which local government has reached may be summarised as follows:

- Most authorities now have a DSO. Generally speaking this is a separate department which acts as the in-house provider of CCT services; in a minority of cases the DSO is a company in which the local authority concerned has a controlling interest.

- A substantial proportion of current CCT contracts have been awarded to 'in-house' bids. At January 1995, nearly 60 per cent of all CCT contracts awarded under the 1988 Act were with DSOs and these contracts accounted for over three-quarters of the total value of work available.

- CCT has generated substantial cost savings, mainly through lower staffing levels but also, to some extent, by reducing pay and conditions of in-house staff.

- The impact of CCT on service quality has been variable.

- CCT has cut across other major legislative changes affecting local government, particularly LMS and local government review. This has increased the complexity of the CCT regulatory framework.

The purpose of this historical background is to demonstrate that:

- CCT now affects a large and increasing number of local authority employees.

- CCT has probably not yet achieved the level of private sector involvement in delivering local authority services that the present Government would have wished.

- The CCT framework is very complicated, and is likely to become more so if the Government continues its campaign to bring more and more services within the CCT umbrella.

The other point to be made by way of introduction is that competition within local authority services is not new – indeed some Council services have faced some private sector competition for a considerable time, e.g. car parking, leisure facilities. In addition, voluntary competition is already well established in some areas. The best example is probably IT, where facilities management agreements are now common.

Even if the impact of CCT does not fully match Government expectations, it is certainly not a transparently cosmetic exercise. It profoundly affects the way in which services have to be managed, both in financial and non-financial terms. Very few managers in local government are totally immune from its influence. The need for some appreciation of what CCT is all about is therefore vital.

In the remainder of this chapter we shall examine the considerable additional demands which CCT places on the management resources of a local authority, and how these demands are being met, particularly on the finance side. The pattern that has now emerged is complicated and is still evolving; this is not surprising given the present Government's determination to reinforce and extend CCT, and the strong political opposition to 'privatisation' which currently prevails in most local authorities. It is very difficult to predict future trends in this area, because they will depend to a great extent on the outcome of the next General Election. However, it would be unwise for local authority managers to assume that an incoming Government, of whatever political complexion, would move quickly to dismantle the CCT framework. The process may well have become a permanent part of the local government scene.

The CCT process

The basic overriding principle of CCT is that a local authority should organise itself so that genuine competition not only exists, but is seen to exist. There has been a widespread acceptance that one of the essential ingredients in achieving genuine competition is a split between the client (purchaser) and contractor (provider). The main structural components of CCT are therefore:

- the client;
- the client agent;
- the DSO (or DLO);
- the DSO Board or Committee.

Each will be considered in turn.

The client

The client is the local authority which is responsible for securing the provision of a particular service. The local authority may be the ultimate recipient of the service, e.g. cleaning of buildings, or there may be another final consumer, e.g. school meals. In its client or purchaser role, the main tasks of the local authority are:

29

- to define the scope of the CCT contract and to specify in detail the service or services to be provided;

- within the statutory limits to determine the duration of the contract and other contract conditions, e.g. use of the authority's premises;

- to implement the contract tendering procedure in accordance with the strict timetable and conditions laid down in CCT legislation;

- to determine the successful tenderer, the assumption being that this will generally be the contractor who can meet the required specification for the lowest price;

- to monitor the performance of the successful contractor, whether in-house or external, to ensure that service delivery is in accordance with the contract specification;

- to meet its contractual obligations in terms of payments to the contractor, variation clauses, default etc.

The client agent

If a particular CCT activity straddles a number of service committees and departments and the local authority does not carry out the client function corporately, it may appoint a particular service committee as the client and the associated service department will then act as client agent for the authority as a whole. The client agent will generally be a department which has relevant expertise of the service(s) concerned, and will be one of the major recipients of the service, e.g. the Education Department for catering services. The client agent will be responsible for enforcing the appropriate standards, and meeting all tender requirements and contractual payments, which will subsequently be recharged to the client.

Our experience is that the client agent role has been one of the most problematic aspects of CCT. This is partly because it has usually been favoured as the least-cost solution, and has therefore been inadequately resourced. It is also doubtful whether a single department, which is seeking to represent the varied interests of several other departments, can be wholly effective in the face of an influential and united DSO.

The DSO

If a CCT contract is awarded in-house, the DSO carries out the work within the specified terms of the tender. Its performance is monitored for quantity and quality by the client, or its agent, and it is required to deliver the service at the price agreed. The contract should include clear procedures for negotiating service variations and for dealing with inflation in costs. The DSO must aim to achieve its financial targets, in terms of turnover, operating cost and profit, over the contract period. It requires financial and other business support, and may have an agreement for the parent local authority to provide some or all of this support. This issue will be covered in more detail later.

The DSO board/committee

Most authorities have established boards or separate committees of elected members to oversee the activities of their DSOs. The precise formats are many and varied, but such bodies are likely to be:

- numerically small;
- representative of all parties;
- comprised of councillors, and advised by a minimum number of officers, typically Chief Executive, CFO, Personnel Officer and the DSO Manager(s).

Their responsibilities could include:

- approving a business plan for the DSO and monitoring its implementation;
- deciding whether a DSO will tender for any particular contract (which may be in-house or external);
- developing appropriate personnel, plant and equipment policies to suit the DSO's operations;
- advising the local authority on distribution/retention of DSO profits.

Overseeing the entire CCT process are a number of agencies, both internal and external, including:

- the CFO of the local authority;
- the external auditor;
- the Secretary of State.

The chief financial officer (CFO)

The CFO has a statutory role, already discussed in Chapter 2, in relation to the financial administration of the local authority. He or she has to be satisfied that safe and efficient arrangements are made for financial affairs and this must include the DSO's affairs as, in most cases, it is still legally part of the local authority. There has to be a financial management framework which takes account of two potentially conflicting requirements:

- from the DSO's viewpoint – providing effective financial support at minimum cost; and

- from the CFO's viewpoint – achieving effective financial control to ensure probity and public accountability.

Both parties should have efficiency and value for money as combined objectives. Subsequent sections of this chapter will discuss how this potential conflict can be minimised.

The external auditor

The role and functions of external audit are covered in Chapter 8. The auditor's certificate and report for the DSO should be separate from those for the rest of the local authority, although it is usual for the same auditor to provide both. The auditor has to report certain matters to the Secretary of State.

The Secretary of State

The enabling legislation, particularly the Local Government Act 1988, gives the Secretary of State extensive powers and considerable discretion to control and extend the CCT regime by issuing statutory regulations. One of the most important provisions within the original Act was the power to set profit targets for DSOs, specified in terms of the return on capital employed (ROCE), and to require a DSO to be wound up if it consistently fails to meet the target. This is not the place to discuss these provisions in detail but it is important to appreciate the considerable legislative pressure on DSOs to achieve prudent and efficient financial management.

During the 1990s, the regulatory powers of the Secretary of State under the 1988 Act have been used both to extend the scope of CCT to 'white-collar' services and to prevent anti-competitive behaviour by local authorities. Both of these issues will be covered in later sections of this chapter.

CCT culture and relationships

It is easy to become engrossed in the detailed structural, procedural and technical changes associated with CCT. Broadly speaking, the most important changes brought about by CCT have been in culture and relationships. These include:

- the emergence of a clear distinction in policy and management terms between the roles of 'purchaser' and 'provider' in relation to Council services;

- recognition that the requirements of the purchaser or client should take precedence over the convenience and security of the provider or contractor;

- a much keener and more continuous interest on the part of managers in cost control, and to some extent quality control;

- a much sharper focus on the cost and quality of support services provided to DSOs.

The purchaser/provider split has now become one of the key issues affecting management structures within local government. Its impact has also extended to the political structure of Councils in so far as different committees now tend to represent the interests of the purchaser (client) and provider (contractor), assuming of course that the latter is in-house.

In management terms, the requirement to establish two separate organisations to achieve what was previously accomplished by one seems an odd way of promoting greater efficiency. Many local authorities started from this sceptical viewpoint in the early 1980s and attempted to operate with at least some of their managers wearing both a client and a DSO hat. Not surprisingly, the problems with this approach were considerable. The tender preparation, submission and evaluation processes are especially difficult for anyone with dual responsibilities. Quality control and performance monitoring have also been fraught with difficulty.

This problem also extends to those activities which underpin CCT services, including and especially finance. In the early days of CCT, 'Chinese walls' abounded in the CFO's department as services to the DSO and the client were redefined and, as far as possible, separated. Data access and security have been a particularly contentious issue. Many DSO managers are extremely unhappy if they find that members of a CFO's staff who provide financial advice to the client have easy access to financial information concerning the DSO.

The partial approaches referred to above have not generally survived into the 1990s and the clear separation of the client and contractor roles for CCT services has now become well established. However, at risk of provoking controversy, it is suggested that this process might in some cases have been taken too far, and that the next few years may see a degree of retrenchment.

CCT is not the only statutory weapon which the Government has brought to bear on local government to encourage a greater 'customer focus'. Much more media attention has been devoted in recent years to the Citizens Charter and performance indicators (*see* Chapter 8). However, it is considered that CCT has had a much greater impact on the way in which local authorities are managed than these more recent initiatives. A significant proportion of the detailed CCT legislation is aimed at allowing market forces to act in the customer's best interests, rather than being outweighed by traditional vested interests on the producer side, particularly political parties and trade unions. LMS has also been very influential in this culture shift, although in a very different way.

DLO and DSO managers face the reality that failure to:

- produce a competitive tender, or

- win the tender, or

- make a profit, or

- meet the Secretary of State's required rate of return,

could ultimately lead to the organisation going out of business and to redundancy for their staff and themselves. It should be no surprise therefore that they are extremely cost conscious, or that they expect prompt information and advice. Finance managers involved directly in providing support to DLOs and DSOs are now fully aware of this challenge, not least because their livelihood is at stake as well. However, it is important that those on the periphery of CCT recognise this new business culture and are prepared for the demands and tensions that it can produce.

The impact of CCT on local government culture and relationships is still evolving as authorities grapple with 'white-collar' CCT and, in some areas, local government reorganisation. Unfortunately, one relationship that has not adapted to the requirements of CCT is that between a local authority DSO and the private sector. Because the DSO is part of its parent local authority, it is limited from competing in the private sector market. Where this limit lies is an issue of continuing debate.

Local authorities' power to trade is covered by the Local Authority (Goods and Services) Act 1970. As well as placing restrictions on the type of organisation with which local authorities can trade, and on the areas of activity in which trading can take place, the Act seeks to define the extent of legitimate trading. The traditional and strict interpretation of this Act has been that trading can only take place to the extent that it utilises surplus capacity within the work-force, which is employed principally for non-trading purposes. A more liberal interpretation of the Act, which now seems to be accepted by Government, but not the Audit Commission, is that local authorities do have the power to trade for profit and to take on staff for the purposes of those trading activities. Although it is providing further gainful employment for the legal profession, this debate is typically confusing for local authorities, and provides only limited encouragement to the entrepreneurial spirit within local government.

Financial management under CCT

In order to operate effectively, the DSO manager will need to be in control of all elements of the DSO budget. Subject to tender requirements and legal restrictions, there should be complete freedom of choice in determining the resources that are employed to achieve the DSO's objectives. Ideally, the DSO manager should not be constrained by:

- traditional local authority personnel policies and practices, including establishment controls over the number and grades of staff who can be employed;

- having access only to the professional and technical advice and support available within the local authority;

- the standing orders and financial regulations under which other local authority managers operate.

It is outside the scope of this book to explore the first of these issues and the subsequent commentary will focus on the second and third points.

In practice, for those DSOs which are still part of the parent authority, the retention of local authority status imposes a number of financial restrictions. Some of these are statutory and include:

- the need for CFO approval to incur capital expenditure unless met from revenue or reserve funds;

- the parallel need for CFO approval to borrow (except possibly on a day-to-day basis);

- the continued right of all employees to belong to the local authority superannuation fund;

- the CFO's control over internal audit arrangements.

Most other financial arrangements within which DSOs operate should be open to negotiation. However, there are a number of areas of financial support to DSOs which are particularly complex and potentially contentious. These include:

- financial systems and the role of IT;
- cash flow;
- financial regulations.

Financial systems and IT

Local authorities are very large organisations. All have computerised financial systems and most are still based on central mainframe applications (*see* Chapter 5). DSOs often require more accessible and up-to-date information and facilities for the local manipulation of data than many central mainframe systems can provide. However, there is still a need to integrate and consolidate the DSO's financial information with that of other parts of the parent authority because of the statutory requirement for the Council as a whole to prepare a budget and final accounts. Therefore, whatever the arrangements for an individual DSO, it will be necessary to provide common or at least consistent information to both the DSO and the centre. This issue is exactly the same in principle as that being tackled as part of LMS and is considered further in the next chapter.

There is also some appetite on the part of DSO managers to carry out the traditional financial management functions in-house, as if they were an independent business. This could include:

- the posting of entries to income and expenditure accounts;
- the provision of costing information;
- the payment of creditors;
- the preparation of income invoices;
- payroll facilities.

If satisfactory local autonomy cannot be achieved by corporate systems, the CFO will have three concerns:

- **Fragmentation**   A DSO decision to abandon a centralised financial system will place an increased burden, in terms of unit costs, on the remaining users.

- **Compatibility**   An alternative financial system may well be unable to provide financial information in the format required to consolidate the accounts without additional effort and cost.

■ **Probity** Each financial system (and there could be several in existence) will display its own problems and inadequacies in relation to levels of internal checks and the effectiveness of control mechanisms.

It is therefore vital that adequate communications and interface facilities exist between central systems and customised local systems. Increasingly, the requirements of CCT are being met by a corporate database feeding networked personal computers (PCs). Typically, there is immediate access to up-to-date information, which is manipulated by flexible spreadsheet and database software. If effectively managed, this can provide information which is highly relevant and easy to interpret.

Charging for IT support has also become more flexible as a result of CCT. This has been necessary to deal with a situation in which a DSO manager can obtain an IT system which will satisfy his or her own needs at a lower cost than the centrally imposed corporate product. It may then be appropriate to levy a reduced IT charge on the DSO, the difference being a corporate overhead.

Financial planning, accountancy and technical support

Business planning is still a relatively new activity for the CFO and his or her staff. It represents a radical departure from the traditional local authority budgetary processes. However it is a crucial aspect in the financial management of DSOs and must therefore be under the direct supervision of the DSO manager. In some authorities a specialised team has been set up within the CFO's department to provide exclusive services to DSO management in this area, and also to support the DSO's budget and final accounts preparation. The need to prepare business plans with:

■ the longer-term perspective required by CCT;

■ the emphasis on outputs rather than exclusively on inputs;

■ in-built performance measures;

■ overall resource requirements, including capital assets;

■ a degree of flexibility;

is a clear example of how the discipline of CCT has stimulated a more businesslike approach across local authorities in general. Departments not yet subject to CCT already have or are in the process of drawing up business plans to enhance their effectiveness, efficiency and long-term survival prospects. Some corporate initiatives with the same business planning focus have also emerged across local government.

An important aspect of financial planning is capital spending for the purposes of enhancing and replacing capital assets. The traditional approaches to local authority asset management and capital accounting are totally inappropriate for CCT. Local authority techniques such as historic cost and debt charges have had to be replaced with private sector concepts such as replacement cost and depreciation. The situation is further complicated in certain tendering situations because the client may opt to retain ownership of the assets employed by the DSO, e.g. school kitchens and catering equipment.

On the accountancy side mention must be made of costing information because this is another area where CCT imposes far greater demands than existed previously. The availability of comprehensive and up-to-date unit cost information is vital to DSO management. Existing financial systems have to be enhanced and interface facilities have to be provided with non-financial databases to enable this information to be produced.

There are a wide variety of technical matters where the DSO managers may look to the CFO for advice and support. These include:

- cash flow;

- insurance;

- VAT;

- National Insurance, sickness and other employee regulations;

- superannuation.

The CFO ought to be in a good position to assist DSOs with their cash flow management because he or she can aggregate all the cash flows of the local authority and provide overdraft and short-term investment facilities at competitive rates. However, DSO managers must be fully aware of their cash flow position and the individual DSOs should receive (or pay) interest relative to their credit (or debit) position. Linked with this is the need for some DSOs to have substantial working capital – another issue which rarely concerns those local authority managers not involved in CCT.

Insurance is a particularly complex issue in relation to CCT. The local authority has a right to expect the DSO to obtain the same level of insurance as the authority itself has – because the ultimate liability lies with the authority. Therefore, the most obvious course is for the authority to apportion its insurance premium(s) between itself and the DSO. If the DSO can obtain a lower quotation for similar risk cover from an external source, then it should pay that premium to the authority but still use the local authority's policy cover. The reasoning here is that most local authority policies are long term and often have discounts built in on the basis that all insurance should be placed with a single company. Where self-insurance is effected, the DSO should again be entitled to pay a lower premium for the appropriate cover, if one can be found in the open market.

There is a tendency for DSO managers and others to regard the local authority status of DSOs as a liability or a handicap. Cash flow and insurance are two examples where the local authority link can be advantageous, because of the economies of scale in these areas of financial managements.

Financial regulations

Most aspects of financial management should be embodied in the local authority's financial regulations. It is convenient to review the operation of financial regulations in the context of CCT and DSOs, although the issue has wider implications. The fact is that recent statutory developments and organisational trends have been pushing in the same general direction, namely towards more flexibility and less detailed prescription in local authority standing orders and financial regulations. Some CFOs may instinctively resist this pressure and, indeed, may be even more determined to retain comprehensive formal controls as budgets are devolved more and more widely. As usual it is a question of balance. The statutory responsibilities of the CFO must be safeguarded, but not at the expense of service quality and, in the case of DSOs, commercial viability.

There is no particular reason why the regulations covering the local authority, DSOs, LMS schools and other establishments should not all be the same – in principle, at least. Only absolute amounts should be different, e.g. limits on virement, bad debt write-offs, etc.

Existing financial regulations are likely to cover:

- accounting and budgeting arrangements;
- capital expenditure and its financing;
- expenditure outside approved budgets;
- virement (switching budget provision between approved budget heads);
- insurance;
- income collection and bad debts;

- internal audit arrangements;

- banking and lending/borrowing arrangements;

- stores and stock accounting;

- provision for carry forwards of expenditure;

- roles and responsibilities of CFOs, service chief officers, DSO managers and establishment heads.

Not all of these headings are relevant to DSOs, e.g. virement. However, there is obvious merit in having a single consolidated set of financial regulations. Flexible financial regulations which are appropriate for DSOs may well form a suitable framework for all local authority activities by the end of the 1990s. In our view the other objectives in adapting financial regulations for the remainder of this decade should be:

- to have a minimum number of regulations with minimal complexity and bureaucracy, and maximum flexibility to respond to changing service needs;

- to assist in maximising the delegation of financial responsibility to the operational level (e.g. the DSO managers);

- to provide effective safeguards in an environment of decentralised financial management, including a formal mechanism for managers outside the CFO's department to report directly to the CFO on financial matters.

The constant review of financial regulations in the light of CCT and other initiatives provides a basis on which it is hoped that financial management in local authorities will develop and from which its ultimate effectiveness will derive. The above comments reflect our basic philosophy. If the will to delegate is there, then the means can be found. Possibly the most controversial of the above objectives is the last one. Is it appropriate to have people reporting to the CFO who may not be accountants and are not on his or her staff? We suggest that the answer is 'yes'. Indeed, in the context of competition, it is our view that this approach provides an opportunity for the DSO or service manager to achieve more effective financial support at lower cost.

Current CCT issues

There are a number of aspects of CCT that are currently active in terms of development and/or debate.

White-collar CCT

The long and tortuous process of extending CCT to 'white-collar' services is at a crucial stage, although it is not easy to explain the situation which has been reached in concise and simple terms.

After a lengthy period of consultation and debate, the start of 1996 saw most of the detailed rules and regulations for white-collar CCT apparently in place, and the process itself well under way. However, it was already becoming apparent that the Government's aspirations regarding the volume of work to be put out to tender, and the degree of private sector penetration into these areas of council work, were unlikely to be fulfilled. Consequently, a further consultation paper appeared suddenly in May, which proposed a number of major changes to the statutory framework. At the time of writing the consultation period for these proposals has not yet expired. However, it seems reasonably safe to assume that the proposed measures will be implemented and the remainder of this section has been written on this basis.

White-collar CCT applies to the following services:

- construction and property services, including the work of architects, engineers, property managers, surveyors and valuers;

- financial services, including local taxation, treasury management, insurance and benefits administration;

- housing management, including rent collection and administering tenancy agreements;

- IT, including telecommunications;

- legal services, including the work of solicitors, barristers, legal executives and licensed conveyancers;

- personnel services, including recruitment, training, staff relations and the personnel aspects of pay, pensions, conditions of employment, health and safety and staff welfare.

It was originally the Government's intention also to subject corporate and administrative services to CCT but this option has now been dropped. The supervision of parking, vehicle management and security are also part of the present tranche of local authority services being opened up to competition.

The precise implementation timetable varies according to the type of authority and has obviously been affected by local government review. It currently spans the period from October 1995 to October 2000.

The other key parameters are the proportion of each of the defined activities which must be subject to competition and the *de minimis* limits, in terms of annual spending on the relevant activity, below which CCT will not apply. These are shown in Table 4.1.

Table 4.1

Activity	Proportion to be subject to CCT (%)	*De minimis* limit
Construction	65	£300 000
Finance	65	£300 000
Housing	95	–
IT	80	£300 000
Legal	45	£300 000
Personnel	40	£300 000

This means that the amount of work which has to be tendered for is the appropriate percentage of the total cost of the defined activity for the year in question, subject to the residual amount being at least the corresponding *de minimis* figure. It should be noted that there is a *de minimis* limit for housing management, but it is more complicated and is based on property numbers. There are also a number of areas of work within each defined activity which may be disregarded, including:

- work paid for by LMS schools from their delegated budgets, and from their devolved allocations for training (GEST);

- work done by employees who spend less than half of their time on the defined activity.

Prior to the latest consultation exercise there were a number of other disregards and allowances which, for many local authorities, would have meant that the amount of work which ultimately had to be tendered for would be very small, or even non-existent! The impact of the new regime remains to be seen.

Anti-competitive behaviour

Quite apart from the difficulties of implementing 'white-collar' CCT, the limited extent to which private contractors have successfully tendered for CCT contracts in general has prompted the Government to highlight and discourage what is seen as anti-competitive behaviour on the part of local authorities. The Secretary of State for the Environment has extensive statutory powers to deal with such activity. A new circular from the Department of the

Environment has recently been issued on this subject. This sets out five principles which authorities should apply in subjecting work to competition, namely:

- ensuring the tendering process is conducted in a fair and transparent manner (in practice this appears to require full and regular reports to elected members both at the tendering stage and during the course of a contract);

- identifying the way in which the market operates for the service in question, and ensuring that the tendering arrangements encourage a good market response (in practice this involves consultation in advance with a range of potential suppliers and relevant professional bodies on the duration and packaging of contracts);

- a focus on outputs, rather than inputs or methods of operation;

- adopting clear procedures for evaluating tenders, which ensure that the required quality can be achieved;

- acting fairly between potential contractors to ensure that the tendering arrangements do not put any one of them at a disadvantage (in practice this is intended to discourage local authorities from withholding relevant information from private contractors, or imposing unreasonable conditions on them).

Although the third and fourth of these principles are the most important, many authorities have already made substantial progress on these fronts. It is the second principle which is likely to be the most problematic in the short term, particularly as it will further extend the already lengthy procedure which must precede the letting of a CCT contract.

TUPE

The Transfer of Undertakings (Protection of Employment) Regulations 1981 (TUPE) seek to protect employees of a local authority or contractor who carry out a defined activity in the event of a different organisation winning the tender for that activity and taking over the contract. It allows the terms, conditions and employment rights of any individuals transferred to the new contractor to be preserved in the short term. The scope of TUPE has been explored at length through the British and European courts, with the inevitable consequence that most of us are now even more uncertain about what is a crucially important aspect of CCT!

Assessment of CCT

It might be assumed from much of the above commentary that CCT has had a wholly beneficial impact on local government services. However, this perception must be subject to at least two major caveats. One concerns the huge complexity of the regulatory framework which now underpins CCT; this inevitably means that much time and effort is expended on the bureaucracy of CCT, rather than on the needs of the community. The introduction of white-collar CCT is a classic example of this. The other question mark concerns service quality. Significant improvements have certainly been achieved in some areas, particularly in relation to measurable performance indicators. However, there are some important aspects of service quality which are not quantifiable, and some of these have been neglected because of the preoccupation with written service specifications, i.e. what can be measured. In addition, CCT has tended to limit the responsiveness and flexibility which was previously the hallmark of some public services.

Any suggestion that CCT has been a panacea would also be open to challenge from the many already low-paid local authority employees who have had to endure a further deterioration in their terms and conditions of employment in order to retain their jobs under the CCT regime. Cleaning and catering staff are probably the prime examples, and it must be remembered that women working part time represent the bulk of this work-force, which poses some awkward questions about equal opportunities!

5

Information technology

KEY POINTS

- Information technology (IT) has the potential to fulfil future management information needs.

- Developments in IT, including those needed to provide decentralised financial information, must be properly planned and adequately resourced.

- Traditional corporate financial information systems (FIS) are inadequate to meet the needs of decentralised financial management, particularly in relation to ease of access and use, flexibility, timeliness and presentation.

- Decentralising of financial management does not necessarily mean the total abandonment of the corporate FIS in favour of the local PC-based systems.

- If a local IT approach, without any direct link to corporate systems, is chosen the resource implications in terms of training, guidance, monitoring and internal audit must be recognised and provided for.

- There needs to be increased attention to the security and privacy issues raised by the developing role of IT in the management of financial information.

Introduction

This book contains a chapter on IT not because local government computer installations have traditionally been part of the CFO's department, but because IT holds the key to future management information needs. As with many other issues covered in this book, this message applies to all areas of local authority management, not just to financial management.

After some general comments about IT development we shall concentrate on financial information systems (FIS) in local authorities. We shall not attempt to cover specialised financial applications such as Council tax collection. These will be crucial to the survival and well-being of all local authorities in the years ahead, but are not, in our view, relevant to the issue of decentralising financial management which is the central theme of this book.

There will be no attempt here to encourage the reader in any particular direction as far as IT is concerned. We do not have the technical expertise to assess the relative merits of mainframes, minis, PCs and other hardware options, or techniques and systems such as networks, databases and spreadsheets, not to mention electronic mail and the Internet. Other important issues into which we will not delve in any detail are:

- the cost of IT and how this should be passed on to users; the advent of networking adds to the existing problems in this area;

- the corporate exchequer (feeder) systems, e.g. payroll, creditors. Their ability to cope with remote interrogation and updating is crucial if they are to support a decentralised approach. Their interface with the corporate FIS may also need to be improved to meet the information needs of decentralised financial management.

What we can do is bring out some of the issues which face managers who are involved in developing information systems to cope with decentralised financial management. Our hope is that this will raise awareness among non-finance managers and also stress to all concerned the importance of a partnership approach to future developments. This is essential if we are to provide information systems which will enable all managers to operate effectively, efficiently and economically in the next millennium.

Managing IT developments

Developments in IT must be based on:

- a clear understanding of information needs;

- careful planning;

- user involvement;

- a flexible approach.

Like financial management, IT is not an end in itself, but merely a means of capturing, storing, analysing and communicating information for management and other purposes. Whenever contemplating IT developments, it is vital to focus on information needs, and to regard systems as 'information' systems, rather than as 'IT' systems. This reduces the risk of being hypnotised by the technology.

In large organisations specific IT developments should generally be planned within the context of a corporate IT strategy. This can be time consuming and frustrating, particularly if the corporate strategy is irrelevant or unclear. A corporate approach does not mean that specific IT developments need necessarily be restricted in the choice of hardware, software or physical configuration. It does, however, mean that they should be properly justified and prioritised on the basis of criteria agreed corporately, and co-ordinated with other developments within the organisation. Local authorities are littered with the debris of *ad hoc* IT developments which were not managed in this way.

At the planning stage it is important to take account of the following factors:

- **Cost**   Many local authorities are severely constrained in undertaking major developments of any sort because of problems with funding. These are the result either of government controls or of concern about the burden on local taxpayers, or both (*see* Appendices B and C). Leasing has been widely employed to overcome the existing capital controls system although this avenue has been progressively blocked in recent years. Operating leases continue to be off-limits under the present capital control system. Direct revenue funding is also free from control, but the impact on Council taxpayers of increases in revenue spending is pronounced.

- **Staff resources**   The availability, or rather the non-availability, of specialist IT staff is a further brake on the pace of IT developments in local government. Authorities have the option of paying the market rates for the necessary staff or of employing external consultants to assist with the design and implementation of new systems. In the case of software, a further option is to purchase an applications package from an outside software house. All these options, of course, have cost implications. It should be noted that IT staff, along with architects and valuers, are the most transferable of all local authority staff to and from the private sector.

- **External solutions**   Irrespective of problems with in-house staff, the purchase of a package from a software house or another organisation may be the most cost-effective solution. It may be that the days are over when individual authorities can insist on individual tailoring of specifications to meet their own needs. This is increasingly the case with standard mainframe applications.

- **Existing IT facilities**   The range of available options may be limited by the existing computer configuration within a local authority. Although it is always technically possible to overcome problems of non-compatibility, the cost of doing so may be prohibitively expensive.

The necessity of involving the end-user in any IT developments is so well accepted that it hardly needs to be mentioned. However, actions do not always match intentions and it is probably fair to say that developments involving financial information systems have a relatively poor track record. This may stem in part from the close proximity of IT staff and finance staff, with the CFO still having responsibility for both groups in many authorities. Managers outside the CFO's department may have been unable or unwilling to participate fully in FIS developments because of this, and undue priority may therefore have been given in the design of financial information systems to the CFO's need for standardisation, consolidation and control at the expense of the non-finance manager's need for clarity, flexibility and accessibility. The spread of decentralised financial management arrangements in some local authorities is highlighting this as a serious deficiency of many corporate financial information systems.

Given a willingness to involve the end-users and, in particular, to establish their requirements at the outset, IT development managers sometimes find initially that users are not sure what they do want. The possibility that user requirements will evolve as an IT development proceeds is one of several reasons why a flexible approach is essential. Another is the likelihood, particularly with developments which have a long lead time, that hardware and/or software improvements will provide opportunities which were not available when the initial evaluation was carried out. A flexible approach will also be necessary to cope with the inevitable delays and malfunctions which are part of any IT development.

The requirements of decentralised financial management

So far we have dealt with general issues which could be applied to any IT project. In the remainder of this chapter we will focus on the demands created by the decentralisation of financial management and how existing financial information systems might be developed to meet them.

What would a service manager with financial management responsibilities expect from a FIS? We suggest that some or all of the following requirements would predominate:

- efficient and economical methods of data capture and storage;

- rapid access to all relevant data, including information in other databases such as property and personnel;

- the ability to manipulate and analyse data to produce useful management information;

- a large measure of control over the format and content of reports and access to facilities such as graphics to enhance presentation;

- the facility to combine text with financial and non-financial information in producing reports;

- automatic generation of key management information and reports;

- a robust, reliable and straightforward system.

Managers in local government are increasingly beginning to question why some of the above facilities are not yet available to them. Moreover they are less willing than before to accept that the improvements which they feel they need cannot be introduced quickly and at low cost. When faced with this sort of pressure, those involved in IT systems development should avoid being panicked into hasty and ill-conceived decisions. Equally they must ensure that, as well as involving users fully in establishing system requirements, they keep users fully informed of progress with design and implementation. If nothing is happening and users are being kept in the dark, they are very likely to seek local solutions without recourse to the IT experts. How often have we seen this happen?

One fundamental issue is likely to recur in reviewing financial information needs as part of any initiative to decentralise financial management. This has already been referred to and concerns the importance of achieving the correct balance between the users' needs outlined above and the CFO's corporate need for standardisation, consolidation and control. Although it is dangerous to generalise it is probably fair to suggest that in most authorities the balance is currently in favour of the CFO's needs. It certainly has been in the past. What is equally certain is that decentralising financial management is shifting the emphasis towards users' needs.

Traditional financial information systems

At present the norm in local government is still for the majority of financial transactions to be processed centrally. This is most evident in the case of the traditional exchequer functions, particularly payroll. The main advantages of the centralised approach are efficiency and probity. In the case of payroll a high degree of expertise is required to cope with the myriad of national pay agreements which cover local authority employees, and the complexities of PAYE, National Insurance, statutory sick pay and maternity pay. It makes sense in efficiency terms for this expertise to be pooled centrally. This approach has also been in tune with the fact that most staffing establishments have until recently been directly controlled from the centre. Reliance on a corporate payroll system using a central mainframe computer has given the CFO's staff firm control over the transactions data covering three-quarters of the authority's revenue spending. Not only is this the best solution in terms of ensuring that all staff are paid correctly and on time; it is also the strongest assurance of the accuracy and integrity of the payroll data which are fed into the FIS. Similar considerations apply to creditor payments and the collection of income, although for these functions the advantages of pooled expertise are not quite so compelling.

Thus the typical local authority model has been and still is of central IT systems for processing payroll, creditor payments, income and other financial transactions fed into a corporate FIS. The purposes of this system are to provide a record of all financial transactions involving the authority in the current and one or more previous years, and to consolidate these transactions in various ways in order to identify both the amounts spent in each establishment or division of service (objective classification) and the amounts spend on each subjective category (employees, premises, transport, running costs, etc.). Budget information is also fed into the system to enable comparisons to be made at various levels between expenditure or income to date and the approved budget for the year. Reports or tabulations are produced weekly or monthly or on request and are distributed to establishments and service departments in order for them to exercise budgetary control. Staff in the CFO's department, and possibly in service departments and larger establishments, will have direct access to FIS via terminals or networked PCs. They will be able to call up a range of standard enquiry screens to assist further with budget monitoring. Special routines are built into the FIS to help close the accounts at the end of each financial year, and there are also facilities within the FIS to assist in preparing the estimates for the forward financial year.

The basis of all such systems is the transaction code. This code contains the information on which the system relies to account for each transaction. Every transaction which is fed into the FIS must therefore have been allocated such a code, which may be 10 or more digits long. Irrespective of any narrative details of the transaction, it is the code on which the IT system will rely to classify the transaction, both in objective terms – where in the organisation the money was spent – and in subjective terms – what the money was spent on.

The corporate FIS therefore relies heavily on a fairly complex and rigid coding structure. Moreover, the integrity of the system is totally dependent on the accuracy with which transactions are coded.

There are two other important characteristics of what might be described as traditional FIS coding structures. One is fairly obvious, namely that codes may not be 'user-friendly' in the sense that there is unlikely to be an obvious link between a code and the objective or subjective nature of the transaction to which it refers. This is not generally a problem for the CFO's staff whose work brings them into regular and frequent contact with the coding structure. However, it may be a problem for staff outside the CFO's department, for many of whom the processing of bills and vouchers is only a very small part of their duties. Pre-printed coding slips and automatic validation checks can be used in certain cases to minimise the problem but it remains the case that many non-finance staff are expected to use a coding system which is far more complicated and obscure than is justified by their own requirements. Perhaps the greatest omission of all is that, in all probability, no one has bothered to explain to them why this is necessary. As decentralised input to central systems becomes the rule rather than the exception, more and more transactions are coded by staff outside the CFO's department and it can therefore be no surprise to learn that dealing with invalid codes and miscodings is a major task for the CFO's staff. This again points to the need for training and awareness raising.

Another increasing problem is that, in most systems, the coding structure defines rigidly the way in which transactions can be analysed and aggregated, and also the coverage and structure of the reports which the system can produce. Aggregation is achieved by identifying all transactions with a common code or part of code. The generation of summaries, sub-totals and totals will therefore be governed by logic of the coding structure. Such problems can be overcome by revising the coding structure but the costs and complexities involved in this sort of exercise are obvious. Special enquiry routines can also be written to cope with this situation but such an approach requires specialist assistance and is inefficient in terms of computer processing resources. The rigid structure of analysis and reporting which is inherent in the traditional FIS is a major weakness when faced with the demands of decentralised financial management.

As well as being inflexible in terms of content, reports from the FIS may well be limited to standard formats. At worst many of the standard formats may be entirely unsuitable for the non-finance manager. At best they may meet the needs of some managers but there will inevitably be others whose requirements cannot be satisfied. We all now understand the importance of presentation in ensuring that management information is understood and properly utilised. Unfortunately this lesson had not been learned when many existing systems were being designed.

The last, but certainly not least, problem with the traditional corporate FIS approach is the timeliness of information which it provides. The defect lies not so much in the system itself but in how and when it acquires some of the transactions data from its feeder systems. A prime example of the problem is expenditure on goods and services. When an establishment manager places an order with a supplier he or she has committed resources from the establishment's budget. By the time the goods have been received, the invoice has arrived at the establishment, the invoice has been passed for payment and the cheque has been produced to reimburse the supplier, a period of several weeks may have elapsed since the order was raised. During that period FIS reports will give an inaccurate picture of the establishment's budget position because the above transaction will not appear in FIS until shortly before the cheque is produced. This will not be the case, of course, if the FIS has an on-line commitments sub-system for recording transactions at the order stage and if that facility has been used by the establishment manager. A commitments facility is now a standard feature of many systems but experience suggests that its use may be patchy; and of course it will be of limited value to any manager who does not have direct terminal access to the FIS.

Our view is that success in decentralising financial management will depend on managers having access to financial information which is easily accessible, flexible in scope and content, up to date and easy to interpret. In many authorities the existing corporate FIS may be seriously deficient in some or all of these respects.

The way forward

In view of the above comments it is important to make clear at this stage our belief that decentralisation of financial management does not necessarily mean the total abandonment of the corporate FIS in favour of decentralised systems to suit local needs. Indeed, it is important not to lose sight of the benefits which retaining a corporate approach to financial information will preserve, namely greater efficiency and higher integrity.

There is little doubt that hardware and software technology is now sufficiently advanced to enable a corporate solution to the information needs of decentralised financial management. Indeed mainframe packages are already on the market which appear to provide the required flexibility of coding, analysis and reporting. Communications facilities are also available to allow any number of outside establishments to have a direct link with the mainframe and therefore immediate access to the FIS and other corporate financial systems such as payroll and creditor payments.

The problems with following this route include the familiar ones of resources and time. All IT developments cost money, take time and require specialist staff resources to plan and implement but those involving mainframe computers seem to consume inordinate amounts of all three. The timetables which the Government set for CCT and LMS were, and continue to be, demanding. There have been other, even more immediate calls on IT development resources in many authorities, such as the implementation of the community charge and, subsequently, the Council tax. Against this background, the approach which seems to have most to commend it is to select a suitable software package from an outside software house. This will at least make it possible to contain within acceptable limits both the time-scale for implementation and the burden on in-house specialist staff. The most sensible attitude in these circumstances is to recognise that perfection is out of reach but that 90 per cent of the ideal may be reasonably cost effective. It is also important to remember that, if this approach is to be attempted, it remains essential to involve users in evaluating the pros and cons of the available packages.

There is no doubt that concerns over the cost and lead time involved in a central solution can only add to the attractiveness of a local solution based on increasingly cheap (in relative terms), sophisticated and powerful PC-based technology. However, it is also fair to suggest that this approach will in any case be more immediately attractive to the end-user for reasons which will range from frustration with corporate systems to hearsay from colleagues in other authorities.

There is an entire spectrum of options for achieving what might be described as the local solution. The extremes are:

- **Local PCs** linked via a network or dial-up facility to the central mainframe. Software provided to download relevant data from the mainframe to spreadsheets or database files. Standard routines provided to analyse data locally and generate reports. Direct access locally to central FIS. Central processing of payroll, creditor payments and income to continue.

- **Stand-alone PCs** Software provided to enable all transactions to be processed and recorded locally, and to enable salary payments and creditor cheques to be generated locally. Local data downloaded periodically on to floppy disks and sent to County/Town Hall to update the central financial database.

The main advantages of the first approach are that it:

- retains the efficiency benefits of central processing;

- requires limited additional expertise and generates only a limited amount of extra administrative work locally; and

- safeguards the integrity of the central FIS.

Its main disadvantages are that:

- there may be less local flexibility than with more radical options;

- the problem of the delay between orders and invoices is not addressed; and

- it is vulnerable to mainframe problems such as slow response or system failure, and to communications problems, particularly if dial-up facilities are used.

The pros and cons of the second approach are a mirror image of the above. Clearly one of the CFO's main concerns must be the extent to which his or her statutory responsibilities can continue to be met. Faced with a local solution of the second type, CFOs will need to:

- review their requirements in terms of financial procedures and information. For example does the CFO need to have a full record of all local transactions or merely a running total of overall spending to date?

- ensure local managers and staff are given adequate financial training and guidance;

- provide clear and comprehensive financial regulations for local managers; and

- increase the resources available to carry out internal audit work in the relevant service areas.

Decentralising financial management responsibilities to local managers will necessitate a considerable amount of training and guidance whatever approach to financial information development is adopted. However, the more radical local solutions to financial information needs will create a much greater immediate training burden because it will be necessary to provide local staff with the expertise and commitment necessary to ensure that transactions are processed and recorded accurately. One of our principal messages is that in the coming years IT developments will enable a continuing decentralisation of traditional financial functions such as creditor payments. Whether more can be achieved, in terms of total management at the point of service delivery, remains to be seen.

Computer security and data protection

The strengths of computerised information systems are that they can handle very large amounts of data efficiently, that data retrieval is fast and easy and that data can be transferred and reproduced speedily and accurately. Increasingly, however, these characteristics are making it ever more difficult to guarantee the security and privacy of such systems.

The best known aspects of computer security are the phenomena of unauthorised access and the computer virus. There is growing media interest in those malicious, but extremely computer literate, people, usually known as a 'hackers' who, either for profit or pleasure, devote much time and effort to gaining illegal access to IT systems. Access protection, by password or other means, is now an essential component in the design of all operating systems and applications software.

If the hacker plants a computer virus in a system, there is a distinct possibility that, at a given moment or trigger, the contaminated system will malfunction or, in extreme cases, self destruct, with possible loss of some or all of the relevant database. As the name suggests, viruses are easily passed on and it is all too easy for many IT systems to become contaminated by the same virus. In the case of PC systems this is always a risk if 'floppy disks' are shared, or used to transfer data from one system to another. Virus-checking software is now available, although this can only search for known viruses. The risk of virus contamination makes it more important than ever to have systematic routines for 'backing up' computer data.

Data privacy is covered by the Data Protection Act 1984, which governs the collection and processing of information held on computers about living people, and is overseen by the Data Protection Registrar. There are eight basic principles, which apply to all computer-based information, as follows:

- personal information must be obtained and processed fairly and lawfully;

- personal data must only be held for specified and lawful purposes;

- personal data must not be used in a way which is incompatible with the specified purpose(s);

- personal data should only be held to the extent that they are adequate, relevant and not excessive in relation to the specified purpose(s);

- all personal data should be accurate and up to date;

- personal data should only be held for as long as is necessary to achieve the specified purpose(s);

- individuals are entitled to be informed by the data user that personal data about them are held, to have reasonable access to those data, and, if appropriate, to have the data corrected or erased;

- appropriate security measures must be taken to prevent unauthorised access to, or alteration, disclosure or destruction of personal data.

There is a statutory requirement for all data users to register with the Data Protection Registrar.

In the local government context it is important to note that, where a statutory duty exists to publish personal data or make it available for inspection, the above requirements do not apply. This was a very important exemption during the period of the community charge register, but is less so under the Council tax.

It is probably fair to claim that, despite some shortcomings, local authorities have a better record of compliance with the Data Protection Act than most of the private sector.

Those who are not sure whether computer security or data protection are relevant to them are strongly advised to assume the worst and seek specialist advice!

6

Financial management functions – exchequer

INTRODUCTION

In the next three chapters we shall describe in more detail the financial management functions listed in Appendix A. We shall concentrate particularly on those functions where decentralisation or contracting out has already taken place or is feasible in the short to medium term. For each of these functions, we shall endeavour to explain in straightforward terms:

- its objectives and component tasks;
- the traditional procedures and problems associated with it.

For the remaining functions we shall confine ourselves to a brief outline of their main purpose and characteristics.

This account will be based entirely on our own experience, which in the recent past has been outside the Finance Department, and so may not reflect the current situation in all local authorities. To minimise the risk of inaccuracy and irrelevance, it has been necessary to restrict ourselves to very general comments.

The present chapter is concerned with exchequer functions.

1 Payroll

The objectives are fairly straightforward, namely to pay the appropriate staff the correct amounts on the due dates. Achieving this in a large organisation with several thousand staff spread across the entire spectrum of professions, trades and working arrangements is a massive and complex commitment.

There are numerous tasks associated with the payroll function. These include:

- dealing with new starters and leavers;

- updating payroll records for changes of address, bank details, etc.;

- statutory deductions from pay – income tax and National Insurance;

- other additions to and deductions from pay, including allowances, superannuation deductions and union subscriptions, attachment of earnings and car loan repayments;

- dealing with temporary variations in pay, including overtime and unpaid leave;

- generating payment by electronic fund transfer (BACS/BACSTEL), crossed cheques to individuals, banks or building societies, open cheques and cash;

- implementing pay awards;

- dealing with annual increments;

- operating the Statutory Sick Pay (SSP) Scheme;

- dealing with maternity leave and pay;

- providing payroll information to the Department of Social Security (DSS), Inland Revenue and Department for Education and Employment (DFEE) (for teachers);

- passing on deductions from pay to DSS, Inland Revenue, DFEE, HM Paymaster General, trade unions and other bodies;

- initiating third-party accident claims whereby compensation for absence from work is claimed from insurers.

For major services the above tasks may be split between payroll staff in the CFO's department and a staffing section in the service department. However, it is not uncommon for the CFO's staff to handle most or all of the above functions for the vast majority of staff.

Computerised payroll systems are now almost universal. The basis of most systems is a payroll master record which is established for each employee and contains all the information necessary for the purposes of calculating the basic pay of that individual, dealing with any permanent variations and determining the frequency and method of payment. These records are held in payroll master files with, generally speaking, each category of staff being treated separately. In newer systems payroll details are combined with other personal details in a comprehensive personnel database. This is obviously more efficient because it avoids key information, such as home address and date of birth, having to be held in separate computer files.

Until recently the most common method of updating the payroll master file and dealing with timesheets and temporary variations in pay was by batch input of dual-purpose forms which are filled in at the establishment or in the service department and are then submitted for data preparation, having first been checked (possibly on a sample basis), and/or completed by the CFO's payroll staff. Several thousand of these forms may arrive in the CFO's department each month. To cope with the large volume of input, the competing demands on computer processing resources and the absolute necessity to pay people on time, strict deadlines must be followed. There will be a separate timetable of deadlines leading up to each weekly or monthly pay-day.

Salaries and wages account for the bulk of local authority revenue spending. It is therefore essential that there are adequate controls within any local authority payroll systems to minimise the risk of loss as a result of error or fraud. Traditional methods of control include:

- proper authorisation of variation forms and input documents;

- manual checking (on a 100 per cent or sample basis);

- exception reports to identify large, unexplained variations;

- control totals for batches and for entire processing runs;

- periodic internal audit scrutiny.

The spread of on-line access to and updating of the central payroll systems from remote locations has created additional security and control problems. Sophisticated systems to control access to payroll data via terminals and micro-computers have been developed to meet this challenge.

The local authority payroll function is fraught with problems. Many of these stem from the high volume and non-uniformity of the transactions involved. Although the majority of local authority employees are now paid monthly by automatic transfer to a bank or building society account, there are still significant numbers of weekly paid staff and, in many authorities, staff who still prefer to be paid by cheque or in cash. A relatively high proportion of local authority employees work part-time, or on a seasonal or termly basis. In a large local authority there will be more than 30 different national and local pay agreements which need to be applied.

Given this complexity and the need for the CFO's staff to rely on data supplied by non-finance staff at service and establishment level, there is a continuous need for training and guidance. Because of the increasing pressure on payroll staff, it is not always possible to meet all the training needs or to keep user manuals up to date. At the same time the heavier burden on managers at the local level could compromise further the quality and timeliness of the source data being provided. This is a resource problem but also a management problem, requiring a clear understanding of priorities and procedures.

2 Creditor payments

Not all organisations pursue the same objectives with respect to the creditor payments function. Particularly for a large organisation, the cash flow implications of reducing the settlement period for invoices by one week are significant. If, as in a medium to large local authority, the average weekly creditors' bill is one million pounds, the interest foregone would be in the region of fifty thousand pounds per annum at current rates of interest. However, the speed with which a large local authority pays its local suppliers is always a sensitive issue politically. We would guess therefore that the primary objective of most local authorities remains to reimburse suppliers promptly and accurately.

Obtaining supplies and services involves the following sequence of events:
- (a) placing an order, verbally or in writing;
- (b) receiving the goods;
- (c) receiving an invoice or bill for the goods;
- (d) paying for the goods received.

All four events may occur simultaneously, as in the case of the purchase of a battery from a local retailer using petty cash. More usually, however, there is a time-lag between each stage in the process. The primary concern of the traditional creditor payments function was to control the operations which link (c), the receipt of the invoice, with stage (d), payment for the goods or services received. However, most larger local authorities also have computerised facilities, linked either with the creditors system, or the FIS, which allow for a commitment to be entered when an order is placed and for the system to be updated as the new order progresses. Indeed, many authorities have gone much further than this and have developed computerised purchase order systems, either alongside or as an integral part of their creditor systems. This enables a much more integrated and efficient approach to the entire procurement operation and provides more useful and up-to-date management information.

There is also considerable variation among local authorities in the extent to which the procedures following receipt of an invoice have been entrusted to service departments and outside establishments. The basic tasks at this stage are:

- To ensure that an invoice is valid and correct. This is achieved by a combination of:

  - local certification by an authorised officer to confirm that the specified goods or services have been received and that the invoice has not previously been paid;

  - bill examination – various levels of check are possible and the extent of checking may depend upon the value of the invoice. The CFO's minimum requirements will specify minimum bill examination checks. This task has traditionally been performed centrally but can be done locally, if the resources and expertise are available.

- To provide the computer with the information necessary to generate a cheque, particularly the name and address of the supplier and the cheque amount. Usually details of all current suppliers are held in a central computer index with each distinct combination of supplier's name and address being allocated a unique creditor number. The appropriate creditor number is entered on a coding slip attached to the invoice along with the invoice amount(s). This task can be done locally as long as there is direct access to the central index.

- To provide basic payment details on the cheque remittance advice so that the recipient can readily identify which amount(s) is/are being settled. This is particularly important if the corporate system is designed to combine all payments to a single creditor into one cheque when carrying out a cheque run. The procedure is sometimes known as detailing.

- To allocate the invoice amounts to the appropriate transaction codes within the FIS. This is already a predominantly local operation with pre-printed coding slips being widely employed.

- To provide an audit trail so that the progress of particular invoices through the system can be followed retrospectively; the simplest way of achieving this is by allocating a unique number to each invoice. In some authorities this is known as a tracer or transaction number.

Coding slips are only required where batch processing is still employed. The alternative is direct input, either centrally or locally.

Apart from certification and bill examination, traditional centralised creditor payments systems generally include other control operations. It is still common for creditor cheque listings to be 'called over' against the original invoices before the cheques are actually produced. Decentralised systems rely on various types of check built into the system software. Although such systems may well allow creditor payments to be recorded and initiated locally, in most cases the cheques are produced centrally. However, recent initiatives, particularly LMS, are encouraging even more radical reviews of present arrangements and local cheque books are now used by many LMS schools.

Decentralisation of the creditor payments function is therefore well advanced in many local authorities. The attendant problems are no different from those involved in decentralising any other financial management function, namely:

- to provide adequate, early and useful information locally;

- to develop economic local procedures for carrying out the tasks involved;

- to provide adequate training (preferably in advance) and guidance;

- to ensure effective financial controls are in place and are applied;

- to feed the corporate FIS and ensure local and central databases are reconciled;

- to provide an audit trail.

The main problems with the existing centralised systems are the high volume of paper which has to be processed and stored, the inflexibility and inefficiency of the older computerised systems and the somewhat unwieldy control procedures which are currently operated in some authorities. These combine to increase the throughput time for invoices and to magnify the difficulties that staff face in dealing with queries from suppliers. The local approach has the potential to avoid most of these problems (although it will still be necessary for invoices to be stored for up to five years to satisfy VAT requirements). This potential will be realised if decentralisation is planned and managed properly over a sensible time-scale.

3 Council tax/housing benefits

Financial assistance to low income families in paying Council tax and housing rents is covered by three types of means-tested benefit – Council tax benefits, rent rebates and rent allowances. The latter two are known collectively as housing benefits. There are statutory schemes covering all three elements. The benefit criteria and levels for each scheme are set by government regulation, although there are a few areas of local discretion. Payments in relation to the statutory schemes are covered by a direct government subsidy of up to 97 per cent. There is also a separate allowance for the cost of administering the statutory schemes which is equivalent to a cash-limited specific grant. Payments and administration costs relating to local schemes do not qualify for subsidy.

In England, the burden of administering Council tax and housing benefits falls exclusively on unitary, district and borough councils, all of which are both billing authorities and housing authorities. The main tasks involved are:

- identifying and advising potential claimants;

- sending out and collecting completed claims forms;

- assessing entitlement to benefits;

- providing benefit to those entitled either through:

   - reductions in Council tax bills (Council tax benefit);

   - reductions in council house rents (rent rebates);

   - cheques to private sector tenants (rent allowances);

- periodically reviewing the circumstances of claimants and reassessing entitlement in the light of any change;

- liaising with the DSS (many claimants are also in receipt of income support);

- completing housing benefit subsidy claims.

This work obviously involves close liaison with the authority's Council tax collection staff and the Housing Department.

The introduction of Council tax to replace the community charge in 1993 required a total revamp of the associated benefit arrangements, the second such upheaval in the space of three years. There have also been periodic major changes to housing benefits since the scheme was first introduced in 1982. The detailed information required by authorities to implement these changes has invariably been supplied by the Government at the last minute. This has caused massive problems, particularly as quite major modifications to assessment procedures and computer systems have often been required.

4 Income

Even if the income from housing rents and other council housing activities is excluded, the total of non-grant income collected by local authorities is currently around £5000 million. Collecting and accounting for such a large sum is a major task. The main objectives here must be the prompt collection, banking and recording of all income due to the authority.

Much of this income is collected locally in the form of cash or cheques at or about the time at which the service is provided. Examples are income from school meals and the use of sports and leisure facilities. Normally the money collected is paid in at a local bank or post office and credited automatically to the authority's bank or National Giro account. Vouchers giving the relevant details have in the past been sent to the CFO's department so that the transactions can be input to the central FIS and reconciled with the authority's bank statements. In larger establishments such as leisure centres, there is an increasing demand for the facility to pay by credit card. Some authorities are resisting this development because of the added procedural complexity. However, the pressure for change will eventually become irresistible and there may be compensating benefits if the availability of credit card facilities reduces the need for debtor accounts to be raised and lessens the physical and security problems associated with cash collection. Increasingly, the transfer of funds between large organisations is being done by electronic fund transfer (BACS).

The other principal method of income collection is usually referred to as the sundry debtors system and involves raising an account for the services provided. Debtor accounts are usually raised in triplicate. The top copy is handed or sent to the individual organisation to whom the services have been provided. It will contain guidance on how payment can be made and often will include a detachable slip which can be enclosed with the appropriate remittance. Of the other copies one will be retained by the department or establishment which raised the account. The remaining copy will be sent to the CFO's department to enable the transaction to be input in the computerised sundry debtors system and, via that system, to be fed into the FIS.

The main functions of traditional sundry debtors systems are:

■ to generate debt recovery action such as reminders automatically at predetermined intervals;

■ to deal with adjustments to accounts and write-offs;

- to cancel the debt when payment is received and to deal with payments by instalments;

- to provide management information to facilitate debt recovery. Such information might include outstanding accounts analysed by individual debtor or by age of debt;

- to provide indication of performance in relation to debt collection and recovery;

- to maintain a record of unallocated receipts – money received which cannot be linked with a specific debt or service provided.

A large number of debtor accounts are raised by the CFO's staff. These are likely to include:

- periodic debts such as rents, wayleaves, easements, school boarding fees;

- accounts for overpayment of salaries or wages where the individual concerned is no longer in employment.

In many authorities debt recovery is hampered by the fact that the FIS is generally updated at the time the debtor account is raised. This means that income is credited to the relevant transaction code before the money is received. This does not provide the department or establishment which raised the account with much of an incentive to chase outstanding debts. As a result debt recovery tends to be given low priority and this serves to increase both the incidence of write-offs and the frequency with which longstanding debts have to be referred to the authority's legal department for recovery action through the courts.

Newer systems allow cash/cheque/credit card income and debt collection to be processed locally. Although such systems, if computerised, may well contain sophisticated checks and controls, their ultimate effectiveness probably stems from the fact that a much clearer link exists between the ability to recover a debt and the amount credited as income in the FIS and ultimately in the accounts.

Council house rent collection is a major financial management function of unitary, district and borough councils in England. In 1995/96 the gross income from housing rents was over £3500 million. Apart from the massive scale of the operation, the other traditional characteristic of rent collection has been the personal visit, both by the rent collector to the tenant and by the tenant to the rent office, as a method of payment. However, more up-to-date payment methods such as direct debit are gradually gaining ground.

Since the introduction of the community charge, council house tenants have settled their local tax liability separately from their rent bill. This is one of many areas where the recent changes in local government finance (*see* Appendix B) have impaired efficiency. On the other hand, the burden of rent collection on local authorities is being progressively reduced by council house sales and the wholesale transfer of housing stock to the private sector under the 1988 Housing Act.

5 Superannuation

In common with many other areas of local government finance, superannuation administration has been affected by major legislation in recent years.

In case of doubt it should perhaps be made clear that the local government superannuation scheme is 'contributory' i.e. individual employees contribute to the scheme through a percentage deduction from their salaries, as well as triggering an employer contribution. Apart from being important from a personal point of view, this is obviously significant in administrative terms.

In the shire areas superannuation administration is based largely at county level and it is the County Council's superannuation section which looks after all the superannuable employees of the district or borough councils within the county. In urban areas, one of the district or borough councils may take a lead role on behalf of all the councils in the area, obviously by agreement with all the participating authorities. In addition to the Local Government Superannuation Scheme which covers most staff, there are separate statutory pension schemes for police and fire brigade staff. It is also necessary for local authority superannuation staff to liaise with the DFEE which administers the teachers' superannuation scheme.

The principal tasks of superannuation staff are:

- dealing with new admissions to one or other of the schemes (generally employees who have recently joined one of the constituent authorities);

- dealing with employees who are moving to authorities outside the area or are leaving local government. This may entail transferring an employee to another superannuation fund or setting up deferred benefit arrangements or, occasionally, a refund of contribution;

- calculating and paying benefits to those eligible, including employees made redundant or granted early retirement;

- advising staff on superannuation matters in general and particularly on the new options now available to them, namely, additional voluntary contributions (AVCs) and the freedom to opt out;

■ promoting the local government superannuation scheme.

As a result of recent legislation, many part-time employees have been brought within the scope of local authority superannuation schemes, and must now be registered unless they specifically choose to opt out. This has caused a substantial increase in membership of all schemes, with a consequential increase in the administrative burden. The promotional aspect has arisen as a direct result of government legislation allowing all employees the freedom to make their own pension arrangements. This means that local authority schemes must be marketed in the same way as similar schemes in the private sector.

Our view would be that, given the specialised and complex nature of superannuation administration, this function should remain under the central control of the CFO for the foreseeable future.

6 Non-domestic rate collection

Under the present system of local government finance, domestic rates no longer exist but local authorities continue to collect rates from business ratepayers. English local authorities collect rates for over 1.6 million business, commercial and other non-domestic properties. Although controlled nationally, this tax is a very important source of local revenue, being worth an estimated £12 700 million to local authorities in 1996/97. Non-domestic rate collection is therefore a substantial commitment for unitary, district and borough councils, which, as billing authorities, are also responsible for the collection of the Council tax.

As described in Appendix B, a uniform national rate is now fixed by Government each year. Billing authorities then produce and despatch rate bills and are responsible for all aspects of collection and recovery. As in the past, rateable values are determined by the District Valuation Office, a branch of the Inland Revenue. Full revaluations now take place every five years. The latest revaluation has just been completed and the new rateable values are being phased in from April 1995.

The amount of business rates collected by a billing authority is not the same as the share of non-domestic rate receipts which is available to finance the spending by the local authorities in its area (*see* Appendix B). Each billing authority is required to maintain a separate collection fund into which all the sums collected in respect of business rates must be paid. The authority makes its contribution to the national non-domestic rate pool from this fund. Income from the national pool is paid to all authorities, whether they are billing authorities or not, and is credited to the general or county fund as appropriate.

There are various key aspects of business rate collection, some of which remain problematic even after five years of the new system. These include:

- the requirement for a revaluation of properties every five years. Although this is preferable to an indefinite gap between revaluations, it imposes a considerable administrative burden on billing authorities, which have to prepare new valuation lists and play a limited role in valuation appeals;

- the even greater importance of distinguishing between domestic and non-domestic property, in circumstances, e.g. holiday homes, where this is far from straightforward (*see also* Appendix B);

- how to deal with losses on collection, i.e. amounts not recovered because of non-payment or as a result of charitable relief and relief for empty properties. Such losses are allowed for in calculating the local contribution to the national pool;

- how to deal with costs of collection – these are borne by the billing authority in the first instance, rather than being charged to the collection fund. However, there is a government allowance towards these costs which is netted off the payment from the collection fund to the national pool. This allowance must be transferred from the collection fund to the general fund;

- transitional arrangements – the effects of measures to phase in the combined effect of the 1990 revaluation and the introduction of the national non-domestic rate are still being felt by some business ratepayers, at a time when a further revaluation has already taken place.

7 Council tax collection

The Council tax is determined locally, subject to capping (*see* Appendix B), and is fixed and collected by billing authorities, i.e. unitary, district and borough councils. In 1996/97, the expected proceeds from the Council tax are £9000 million.

One of the reasons for the failure of the community charge was its administrative complexity, and experience to date with the Council tax has confirmed that it is much less problematic to administer. However, the relative ease with which the Council tax has been implemented owes much to the expertise and commitment of the local authority staff involved, and it would be a mistake to assume that Council tax administration is entirely problem free.

The principal characteristics of the new system are outlined in Appendix B. In terms of administration, the key issues include:

- setting the tax, which basically involves calculating the Council tax base, fixing the budget requirement, assessing the amounts due in respect of revenue support grant and the national non-domestic rate and determining the requirements of precepting authorities;

- the development of sophisticated computer systems to deal with all aspects of Council tax collection;

- payment by instalments – annual bills are normally paid by 10 consecutive monthly instalments, although, in the case of council house tenants, more frequent instalments can be arranged to coincide with rent collection dates;

- payment methods – these include direct debits, standing orders and bank giro credits, via post office, bank or building society, and cheque or cash direct to the billing authority. Many authorities now offer facilities for payment by credit card and some also operate savings stamp schemes, similar to that for TV licences;

- enforcement – if an instalment is not paid in full by the due date a reminder notice must be issued, giving seven days for the outstanding instalment(s) to be paid; if this is not complied with, the right to pay by instalments is lost and the full balance of the year's Council tax becomes due. Default on payment can lead to a court summons, a liability order, an attachment of earnings order, a distress warrant and, ultimately, imprisonment.

The collection fund which was referred to above is also used to deal with many of the receipts and payments in respect of the Council tax. All sums received from Council taxpayers are paid into the collection fund, as is the Government subsidy for Council tax benefits. Precept payments to major precepting authorities, e.g. county councils, police authorities, are paid out of the fund. Precepts to parish and town councils are actually paid out of the general fund of the billing authority concerned. The costs of Council tax collection are also met from the general fund of the billing authority. Collection fund surpluses or deficits are shared between the billing authority and its major precepting authorities.

It is important to remember that billing authorities are still having to deal with the aftermath of the community charge. In particular, poll tax arrears are still being collected and these must be accounted for through the collection fund.

8 VAT administration

Although local authorities do not, in the main, bear VAT, there must be a system in place to account for all the VAT which an authority has paid to those of its suppliers who are standard rated. This amount can then be reclaimed from HM Customs and Excise.

In addition certain local authority services, particularly those that are provided in parallel with the private sector, are liable for VAT. Car parking and trade refuse collection are obvious examples. It is essential to ensure that suitable arrangements exist for collecting and accounting for the appropriate amounts of VAT.

The need for VAT expertise within local government was heightened by the introduction of penalties for errors in monthly VAT returns. Errors can now lead to a 'serious misdeclaration' surcharge of 30 per cent of the error plus interest. In addition the 1989 Finance Act extended the coverage of VAT to some areas of construction work and to certain transactions involving the sale or letting of land and/or property.

The limited scope and specialised nature of VAT administration, plus the need for VAT returns to be provided on a corporate basis, means there is little point in locating this particular function outside the CFO's department.

9 Risk management and insurance

Local authorities own large amounts of property and equipment. They also employ large numbers of people. Last, and by no means least, they have frequent and regular contact with the general public, both as direct service providers, and as regulatory and advisory bodies.

The wide spectrum of day-to-day activities in which local authorities are involved gives rise to various risks, many of which are insurable. The main categories of risk are:

- **property** – loss, destruction or damage;
- **liability** – the effects of error, omission, fraud or negligence;

- **motor** – death/injury to employees and third parties, plus damage.

There is now a clear recognition in local government that the primary aim should be to minimise risk. Risk management, as this activity is now called, is a responsibility of all local authority managers. However, awareness-raising, training and expert guidance still tend to be left very much to the insurance officer, who is usually based within the CFO's department. The other tasks of the insurance officer and his or her staff are to:

- review periodically the range and level of insurance cover. In a large organisation it may well be a realistic option to do without insurance cover for certain categories of risk;

- negotiate with external insurers to obtain the desired cover on the most favourable terms. Most authorities carry out a periodic tendering exercise;

- manage the insurance fund, if one exists;

- deal with all insurance claims affecting the authority, in consultation with the appropriate service department and, sometimes, the legal department.

By establishing an insurance fund, an authority can exercise a degree of self-insurance. Such a fund is established initially by means of a lump sum contribution from the centre. The fund's resources are then used to meet claims in certain specific risk areas, e.g. motor vehicles. The relevant establishments and services are charged premiums for the cover provided and these are paid into the fund. If properly managed, the fund will grow over time and this will enable self-insurance to be expanded. The underlying purpose is to obtain the most cost-effective insurance cover by improving cash flow and avoiding the profit margin applied by external insurers.

As conventional insurance cover becomes increasingly expensive a new approach in larger local authorities is to combine risk management and self-insurance with stop-loss cover. Under this type of arrangement the authority covers all the risks itself unless the losses exceed a given threshold (usually quite high). The threshold may apply to a financial year or to a single event. Alternatively, there may be a separate threshold for each.

Insurance is another financial management function where the advantages of a corporate approach and the degree of expertise required make it difficult to envisage decentralisation to any significant extent. However, it is very important that there is a high awareness of, and strong commitment to, risk management throughout the organisation.

7

Financial management functions – co-ordination, control and accountability

1 Financial planning

In recent years it has been very difficult for local authorities to engage in sensible forward planning, mainly because of the financial constraints and uncertainties created by government intervention. The gradual resurgence of strategic planning has come about, not because the situation is becoming easier, but because local authorities are recognising that a flexible business plan with clear objectives, priorities and resource options is essential to maximise effectiveness. It also reflects:

- a strong desire to identify and meet the needs of the community – this requires both research and planning;

- the impact of legislation which is forcing local authorities to decentralise detailed managerial responsibility and therefore requiring a strategic approach to policy-making.

The preferred outcome of a strategic planning exercise would in our view be:

- a prioritised statement of achievable objectives taking account of:

  - statutory commitments;

  - local needs and circumstances;

  - elected members' policy requirements;

- a plan setting out in resource terms how these objectives will be achieved. This should include an allocation of both capital and revenue resources over broad service areas for the period of the plan;

- statements indicating the underlying assumptions on which the plan has been based and identifying any factors which cannot be quantified but which may hamper achievement of the plan. Trends in inflation, interest rates and government grant are obvious examples.

A strategic plan is insufficient on its own for detailed policy implementation. In addition there is a statutory requirement for local authorities to produce annual revenue budgets so that levels of local taxation can be determined.

1.1 Annual revenue budget

Given the financial restrictions and uncertainties which have preoccupied local authorities in recent years, it is not surprising that the annual revenue budget has generally been the predominant vehicle for policy planning and implementation in local authorities.

The annual revenue budget or estimates process is a long-established and reasonably familiar exercise in all local authorities. At one time and in some authorities, the preparation of revenue estimates was an exclusive preserve of the CFO. The norm these days is very much for service departments to prepare the detailed estimates and for the CFO's staff to:

- exercise a co-ordinating and advisory role to ensure accuracy and consistency;

- deal with areas of the budget which are outside service department control, e.g. support service recharges, capital financing costs, contingencies.

At present local authority annual revenue budgets are statements of resource inputs, possibly supplemented by lists of objectives and statistical comparisons, both between authorities and also over time, of service levels and standards. As the 1990s advance, the emphasis in some authorities is shifting towards target performance levels for each specific activity along with a statement, containing only appropriate detail, of anticipated resource costs. For the moment, however, input budgeting remains the predominant approach.

The annual revenue budget can be drawn up in a variety of ways:

- zero based;

- continuation;

- commitment;

- cash limited.

It is important for non-finance managers to appreciate how these approaches differ both in their rationale and as to their suitability in practice.

Zero-based budgeting

Zero-based budgeting (ZBB) is a method whereby an entire activity or area of the budget is examined in relation to its objectives and a comprehensive review is undertaken of the full range of available options for achieving those objectives. It is often described as a 'needs-led' or 'root and branch' approach. Theoretically it is the most satisfactory approach to budgeting because it questions every aspect of the activity under scrutiny. However, it is extremely time consuming and could not be undertaken every year for any of the major local authority services without a substantial input of staff resources, both by the CFO's department and by the relevant service department. An alternative approach, is to subject each service to a ZBB review every (say) five years. In the intervening years one of the other budgetary approaches described below would be used.

Continuation (or incremental) budgeting

Continuation budgeting is a widely used system which attempts to identify the level of spending which would be required in the forward year to continue existing policies and standards of service provision. This allows an incremental approach with the following marginal adjustments being applied to the current year or base budget:

- **full year effects** – to take account of policies or changes in activity which have been introduced part way through the current year;

- **once-and-for-all items** – one-off items of expenditure or income in the current year;

- **demographic trends** – expected changes in client numbers, e.g. school pupils;

- **statutory requirements** – the unavoidable impact of new legislation which may necessitate additional or reduced spending;

- **revenue consequences of the capital programme** – extra revenue costs generated by capital projects, including additional operating costs as well as capital financing costs;

- **inflation** – the estimated cost of pay awards, price increases and trends in interest rates.

The main advantages of the continuation budget approach are that its rationale is well understood and accepted, particularly by non-finance managers, and that it provides a suitable base from which to make policy changes in either direction. Its problems are those of interpretation and consistency. There is a host of different ways in which the continuation of present policies can be interpreted and this leads to both inconsistency and disagreement, usually between the CFO's staff and service department managers. One area of frequent controversy is the extent to which the withdrawal of central government funding for specific projects can be allowed for in the continuation budget. This problem stems from the Government's inclination to 'pump prime' initiatives by targeting specific grant support during the planning and implementation stage which is subsequently withdrawn, once the initiative has been developed.

Commitment budgeting

An approach which has commanded some support in recent years, as financial constraints have really begun to bite, is the commitment approach to budgeting. A commitment budget will invariably be less than a continuation budget because the former will exclude activities which are discretionary in nature. Although this is an easy enough concept to grasp, it is very difficult to define clearly. Where is the line to be drawn? To restrict commitment budgets to activities where there is a clear statutory duty would surely be unduly harsh. Agreed definitions and boundaries need to be established at the outset.

Cash-limited budgeting

The essence of this approach is the acceptance that policy planning and implementation must be finance led. This is the approach employed by the Government in managing its own departments and in attempting to control local authority revenue spending through the grants system. It is conceptually simple. The forward year's budget for a particular service area is fixed in volume terms, possibly using one of the other budgeting methods described above. An allowance is added for anticipated inflation and the service then has to be managed within the overall cash limit. This is an effective procedure for delivering budgets on target but is usually more difficult to manage at the service level than the established continuation approach.

To combine strategic planning with a global ZBB approach to the annual revenue budget would appear both wasteful and unworkable. What the 1990s has seen is less reliance on the traditional line-by-line continuation budget approach to local authority financial planning and a shift towards:

- a medium-term strategy covering three or more years;

- a less detailed annual revenue budget geared to the objectives, commitments and priorities identified in the medium-term plan;

- cash limits combined with wider powers of virement (transfer between budget heads);

- increased flexibility between years, e.g. automatic carry forward of unspent budget provision (within specified limits);

- performance targets for at least some areas of the budget;

- a rolling programme of ZBB or other in-depth service review.

1.2 Capital budgeting

Non-finance managers' familiarity with the annual revenue budget process does not usually extend to the area of capital budgeting. There are a number of reasons for this. Capital projects tend to be very expensive and to span more than one year. Major projects often have distinct stages, such as:

- feasibility and design;

- land acquisition;

- site preparation;

- construction;

- equipment installation;

- landscaping.

Each project must be painstakingly planned, and the figures in the capital programme showing the estimated payments flow for a particular project are usually the outcome of a major corporate exercise.

Other characteristics of capital spending are equally important in encouraging a centralised approach to capital budgeting. Principal among these are:

- the choice of financing methods;

- capital control implications.

These are explained in Appendix C. Limitations on local authority capital spending in recent years have made a corporate approach to capital budgeting essential. It is significant that schemes intended to decentralise decision-making, such as LMS, have specifically excluded capital spending from the delegation process.

2 Budgetary control

The preoccupation with resource inputs rather than outputs, the highly centralised structure of most local authorities and the emphasis on probity and accountability have all contributed to a conservative approach to budgetary control in local government. Generally speaking, budgetary control is and always has been an exercise purely to contain actual expenditure within the budget provided, both in overall terms and at the detailed level.

To facilitate this task budget holders are generally provided with monthly tabulations produced by the FIS. These show details of expenditure and income to date for each budget line and compare these with the approved budget. A standard budget monitoring report will have a separate line for each budget head with separate columns showing:

- transaction code;

- narrative description, e.g. caretakers' salaries;

- expenditure in the current month (and possibly expenditure in one or two previous months as well);

- expenditure to date in the current financial year;

- approved budget;

- variance from budget expressed in both cash and percentage terms.

Some systems are able to display expenditure at the same stage in the previous year and to compare that with out-turn expenditure for the year.

Such reports contain a great deal of information and much of it is very useful. Indeed it is fair to argue that many budget holders do not make the fullest use of their budget monitoring reports. The first step to improving budgetary control may be to provide budget holders with basic training in how to interpret and utilise these reports.

However, it must also be said that monthly tabulations are often cumbersome, poorly laid out, unduly cluttered with figures and, above all, out of date. Some of the information contained in these reports is probably irrelevant to the budget holder because it relates to budget lines such as repairs to premises, administrative recharges and capital financing costs, over which he or she has no direct control. Moreover, many of these budget lines show nil expenditure until the year end. This distorts comparisons between budget and actual spending to date for the establishment or service as a whole.

As explained in Chapter 5, the FIS, and hence the reports produced from it, will not give an up-to-date picture of invoices passed for payment unless a commitments system is available and is used. Another reason why monitoring reports are often out of date by the time they reach budget holders is simply that it takes several days, if not a week, to print, separate and distribute them, particularly in large organisations where month-end tabulations are generated automatically for all budget holders at the same time.

There are several obvious improvements that can be made to this sort of system. These include:

- limiting reports to controllable budget heads only;

- including commitments, if possible;

- reducing the number of columns;

- rounding numbers as far as possible to reduce clutter;

- highlighting areas of concern, e.g. overspends;

- providing exception reports, i.e. only showing budgets which are overspent.

Non-finance managers who have to suffer the present shortcomings and have no alternative sources of budgetary control information, such as on-line access, are entitled to complain and press for improvements. Further sophistication is possible. Comparing the current situation with the position at the same stage in the previous year is a very useful and straightforward budgetary control technique which has already been mentioned. Budget profiling is a substantial refinement which is becoming increasingly available. For areas of the budget where there are seasonal fluctuations a non-linear profile of anticipated expenditure through the year is defined and compared with actual spending to date. For example a quarterly budget profile for electricity might be as shown in Table 7.1.

Table 7.1

	Percentage of year elapsed	Expected percentage of budget spent
June	25	15
September	50	25
December	75	60
March	100	100

In the absence of profiling, the electricity budget would normally appear underspent until the very end of the financial year. It is significant that we have consistently referred to budget **monitoring** reports rather than budgetary **control** reports. Management information of this sort provides a basis for decision-making but it does not guarantee that management action will take place. It is important therefore not to confuse budget monitoring with budgetary control. The latter can only be effective if appropriate corrective action is taken when the need arises, i.e. when a significant budget variance occurs or appears likely. This may take the form of a budget overspend, but this need not be so. Underspending can undermine an authority's policy objectives and plans every bit as much as overspending.

When budgetary control is viewed in this way, i.e. as a process of monitoring, evaluation and action, it becomes an integral part of the management process described in Chapter 1. It also brings conventional budgetary control much closer to the process which is likely to succeed it by the year 2000, namely performance review. The weak link is still the limited ability to focus on output rather than input.

3 Final accounts

Local authorities have a statutory duty to prepare annual accounts for each financial year. These are subject to audit by an external auditor appointed by the Audit Commission. There are a variety of statutory requirements and codes of practice governing:

- the separate statements which have to be produced;

- the format and content of these statements;

- the timetable and procedures which have to be followed with regard to publication and public scrutiny of the accounts;

- external audit requirements and procedures.

It is not the purpose of this book to describe in detail the statutory framework within which local authority final accounts, are prepared and published. Closing the accounts, the process which culminates in the publication of the final accounts is a complex technical exercise which is directly linked with the CFO's statutory responsibilities (*see* Chapter 2). Although staff in service departments and establishments inevitably play an important part in the exercise, the role of co-ordinating and consolidating the process is a core financial function.

4 Statutory reports and returns

4.1 Statutory financial returns

All local authority departments are involved in compiling and submitting statutory returns and the CFO's department is certainly no exception. The most important statutory financial returns which authorities have to render are:

- **Return of expenditure and rates (RER)**   an annual return produced in March/April which provides detailed information on the authority's annual revenue budget.

- **Revenue out-turn/capital out-turn (RO/CO) forms**   This is also an annual return and is completed during July as part of the closing programme. It records out-turn spending for each service area on both revenue and capital account.

Changes in format and coverage of statutory returns are a recurring problem and make it especially difficult to automate the compilation process.

4.2 Annual report

Although the annual report and the statement of accounts (final accounts) are often combined in a single publication, they are separate entities with distinct objectives. Local authority annual reports are produced in accordance with a separate code of practice whose stated objectives are:

- to give Council taxpayers clear information about local government's activities;

- to make it easier for electors, Council taxpayers and other interested parties to make comparisons of and judgements on the performance of their authorities;

- to help councillors form judgements about the performance of their own authority.

The code of practice specifies in some detail the information, both financial and non-financial, which should appear in an authority's annual report. There is also a requirement for general statistics on the scale, usage and cost of services, and specific key service indicators (such as cost per pupil) to be included along with comparative figures for previous years and/or other authorities.

There is now a wide variety of annual report formats in local government. An increasingly popular approach is the newspaper format which can be subsidised by advertising and therefore provides an opportunity for the report to be given wide circulation within the authority's area without undue expense. The CFO's staff now play a more limited though important part in producing the annual report.

4.3 Council tax notices

There is yet another set of statutory regulations governing the information which must be included on Council tax bills or accompany them. Most of the required information is financial and is therefore provided by the CFO's staff. Information must be provided both for the billing authority itself and for any major precepting authorities. This can be done either by distributing separate leaflets or by incorporating the required precepting authority's figures in the leaflets produced by each billing authority.

5 Grant claims and external funding

As well as being disturbing from the point of view of local autonomy, the increasing resort by central government to specific grants has led to a growth in the burden of grant claims. The work involved may be considerable and is often shared between the CFO's department and the relevant service department.

Although most of the spending information required for the purposes of calculating revenue support grant has in the past been extracted by the Department of Environment from RER and RO forms (see above), a large variety of demographic and other non-financial data are used to calculate standard spending assessments (SSAs) for each authority (see Appendix B). Some of the required data are extracted from existing returns – such as Form 7 for school pupils. It is therefore important for non-finance managers to be aware of the potential significance of these statistics and the need for accuracy in compiling them. For example, each secondary school pupil over the age of 16 is currently worth around £3000 of SSA and grant.

The philosophy and impact of external funding, e.g. single regeneration budget (SRB), European Union (EU) grants, are discussed in Chapter 9. The mechanics of bidding for external funding are generally complicated and longwinded, as well as being potentially wasteful. For example the bidding process for the first round of SRB is estimated to have cost £14 million.

Similarly, it was reported recently that 70 European Regional Development Fund (ERDF) projects were still awaiting consideration, a full year after they were submitted. Delays of this sort are very difficult to cope with, particularly if a bid is reliant on matching local funding, which is invariably the case.

The bidding culture has generated its own growth industry concerned with preparing and presenting bids, not to mention lobbying. Whether it has helped authorities to meet the needs of their local communities is another matter.

6 Cash flow management

Cash flow is the CFO's professional responsibility. In most larger local authorities there is an officer who spends all or a significant part of his or her time liaising with the money market and the banking institutions in order to try to maximise the day-to-day cash position of the authority. If one examines a local authority's estimates in some depth, figures will be seen of interest payable and receivable, which amount to several million pounds per annum. The cash flow manager's performance is measured by the size of those figures, and the relationship between them.

Cash flow management operates as follows. An estimate is made each day – or several times in a day on occasions – of whether the authority requires to borrow money to fund its requirements, or whether there is a surplus of cash. Suppose a cash deficiency of one million pounds is identified. There are then two issues to be decided. First, an effort is made to estimate how long the deficiency will persist, e.g. overnight, a week, a month, more than a month. This presupposes the authority has cash balance forecasts sufficiently far ahead. Most authorities have a weekly forecast for a year ahead, and a daily one for a month ahead.

Having established how long the one million pounds will be needed – say seven days – the cash flow manager then enters the market place, by contacting the authority's money brokers, a city institution which should know where the best borrowing rates can be obtained. It is also usual to contact a few financial institutions with whom the authority deals frequently. Doing so may well secure a better rate and save the expense of brokerage fees. When the best rate is identified, the deal is made and one million pounds is transferred from, say, a building society to the authority's account at a clearing bank. It is repaid seven days later.

The opposite happens if there is a surplus of cash. The authority also has a list of financial institutions or types of institution to which it will lend. Due care is needed in choosing a borrower. For the sake of prudence and safety it is not thought worthwhile to risk a very large sum of money for an extra 1/16 per cent on the rate of interest with some of the less well-known secondary financial institutions. Of course, an authority will accept anyone as a lender. The choice of borrower is at present up to each authority's individual judgement, although since 1990/91 lending to a non-authorised body has not been allowed.

More recently an argument has been developing about the desirability of individual local authority establishments with delegated powers and responsibilities being allowed to manage their own cash flow.

There are two aspects of cash flow management:

■ the cash flow effects of management action, e.g. more effective debt collection improves cash flow;

■ the ability to decide how and when to invest and borrow.

In theory both aspects of cash flow should be delegated because establishment management should embrace control over as many resources as practicable. However, the financial benefits of leaving the second element of cash flow management at the centre are enormous. Not only will the amount of cash to be invested or borrowed be much more accurately determined, but the negotiating position will be vastly superior because large sums will be involved. Our own view would be that the costs to the local authority of decentralising this aspect of cash flow management will be significantly greater than any benefits which may accrue in time.

7 Debt management

Like cash flow, and very closely related to it, borrowing is also a professional duty of the CFO. Borrowing embraces the entire spectrum from overnight borrowing on overdraft from the authority's own bank to a 25 year loan from the Public Works Loan Board (PWLB). It is a prime function of a CFO to attempt to create a portfolio or framework of borrowing arrangements which will be to the financial benefit of the local authority.

These few paragraphs cannot do more than touch on what is a highly technical and complex area. It might be worth noting that many large private sector organisations advertise for group or corporate treasurers at rates of pay in excess of those of most CFOs. Their duties are very largely cash flow and borrowing, matters which take up about 1 per cent of the content of this book!

There are some fundamental principles that CFOs must consider when examining borrowing requirements:

- the availability of other internal funds;

- the structure of interest rates for different periods of time;

- the future trend of interest rates – in the short and longer term;

- the fixed and variable instruments that are on the market;

- the PWLB conditions and maximum borrowing levels;

- the various limits placed by statutory instruments on temporary borrowing;

- the redemption period for borrowing; it is not in the interest of the authority for all borrowings to mature at the same time in case interest rates are very high then.

As a result of prolonged creative accounting in the face of Government spending restrictions, some local authorities now have very limited scope to reorganise their portfolio of debt in a way which will lessen the burden of debt repayments, even in the short term. However a wide variety of negotiable and fixed forms of borrowing is now available to accommodate almost any needs. New instruments are continually arriving on the market and city-based specialist advisers are increasingly necessary to help CFOs understand what is available.

8

Financial management functions – audit, commercial, information and advice

1 Audit

1.1 Internal audit

The Chartered Institute of Public Finance and Accountancy (CIPFA) has defined internal audit as 'an *independent* appraisal function within an organisation for the *review* of activities as a service to all levels of *management'*. The key words have been italicised. Audit is a financially based independent review function and internal audit is a service to management. Those non-finance managers who have only experienced the traditional 'ticking and checking' approach to internal audit may find this difficult to accept but let us hope that they are now in a significant minority.

There is a statutory duty on each local authority to maintain an 'adequate and effective internal audit' and this responsibility is invariably vested in the CFO. Recognised guidelines exist which spell out this duty in more detail. They require the internal auditor to monitor:

- the effectiveness of routine managerial controls;

- the custody and security of assets; and

- the adequacy of management information.

Clearly it is impossible for a limited number of staff based in the CFO's department to monitor directly and continuously all areas of activity within a large, diverse and dispersed organisation such as a local authority. Internal audit work must therefore be planned. The objectives of internal audit plans are to establish audit priorities and to ensure the effective use of audit resources.

Audit priorities can be assessed by examining two key aspects of all financial systems:

- materiallty;

- risk.

Materiality is easier to measure. For example, a payroll system which processes transactions with an annual value of £100 million is clearly more material than a petty cash account in a small primary school. Assessing risk is more difficult. Where systems-based auditing is used (*see* below) previous audit findings can be used to identify systems where the risk of a loss occurring is high, but often the auditor has to rely largely on his or her professional expertise and experience. Indices of risk can be combined with materiality, usually expressed as turnover per annum, to give an estimate of the potential loss in each area of activity in a given period. Where the potential loss exceeds a certain benchmark (say £10,000 per year) it may be decided to review the systems annually. If the potential loss is less than (say) £500 per year, the system may not be reviewed at all. This enables the audit plan to be drawn up.

Within local government, there are three accepted internal audit approaches:

- **Transactions auditing**   This is the most traditional audit approach and is based on the principle that the validity, accuracy and completeness of an organisation's financial transactions can best be confirmed by an examination of the originating or prime documents. In practice, it is the most reliable approach but also the most cumbersome and the work involved can prove boring and routine. It does not encourage initiative and tends to result in internal audit sections requiring large numbers of staff. Nevertheless, some transactions are so important that they will always have to be audited.

- **Systems auditing**   This approach arrived in the mid-1970s from North America. It is based on the principle that most financial transactions pass through a system of controls designed to confirm their validity, accuracy and completeness. The controls provide the checks normally carried out by the auditor when performing a transactions audit. It is not necessary therefore to check so many transactions if it can be confirmed that the system contains all the necessary controls and that these are operating correctly. Once the initial documentation and evaluation of system controls have been completed, this approach requires a much lower level of audit resources than does transactions auditing. However, the initial workload is substantial and requires a high level of expertise. Consequently, the approach is not yet well developed.

- **Systems-based auditing** Fortunately, some organisations did persevere with systems auditing and in the late 1970s developed from it the technique of systems-based auditing which is now used in many organisations in the public and private sectors. This approach involves the documentation of system controls only (rather than the flow of documents through the system). It:

  - introduces the concept of 'key controls';

  - enables the internal auditor to rely upon the findings in previous audit reviews when assessing risk areas in the audit planning process;

  - considers the interrelationship of systems;

  - requires the auditor to take a wider managerial view of audit findings.

  In practice this approach requires a considerable amount of thought and a fairly low level of detailed checking. It is essentially a risk-based approach to internal auditing.

Internal audit plans must be flexible. Incidents occur during the period of the plan which were not foreseen when the plan was produced but which require immediate audit attention. The obvious example is an incident of suspected theft or fraud. Audit plans should include a margin for unplanned audit work but this may well not be sufficient.

The scope for decentralising the internal audit function is discussed in Chapter 2. The key issue is probably that of independence. However, it must be recognised that retaining internal audit work entirely within the CFO's department as a core function may achieve total independence at a high cost in terms of audit effectiveness as a service to management. Indeed the traditional view of audit independence is becoming increasingly difficult to sustain as a result of the rapid pace of development and the resource difficulties which most local authorities face. This will be a major issue for debate during the remainder of the 1990s.

1.2 External audit

The Audit Commission for Local Authorities in England and Wales was established by statute in the early 1980s. The Commission is responsible to the Government for the audit of local authorities and has complete control over the appointment of external auditors. Currently local authorities are audited either by officers of the District Audit Service, the public body which previously had a near monopoly of local government audit, or by representatives of private sector accountancy firms. Fees charged to authorities for external audit are fixed by the Audit Commission after consultation with the local authority associations.

External audit work is governed by the Local Government Finance Act 1982, which set up the Audit Commission, a Code of Audit Practice (which has recently been revised) and the Accounts and Audit Regulations, which are also in the process of being modified (see Chapter 2).

The principal duty of the external auditor is to express a formal audit opinion on the statement of accounts. He or she is required to certify that the statement of accounts 'presents fairly' the financial position of the authority. If the auditor is not satisfied on any of the matters on which this opinion has to be based, the audit opinion should be 'qualified'. This rarely happens in practice because potential criticism is usually resolved by agreement before this stage is reached. Where there are areas of concern which do not justify qualification the auditor may make a report in the public interest or include them in a management letter at the conclusion of the audit. In addition to providing an audit opinion, the Code of Audit Practice identifies a number of other key audit objectives, including:

- value for money;

- prevention of fraud and corruption;

- collection and publication of 'profile' information and, more recently, performance indicators.

A major task of the Audit Commission, since its inception, has been the promotion of value for money (VFM) in local government. The Commission has carried out and sponsored a variety of VFM studies in particular service areas and has invariably managed to identify significant potential savings. The value of some of this work has been undermined by the Government's eagerness to make immediate global reductions in its spending forecasts and grant provision on the basis of the Commission's findings.

During the first half of the 1990s, the other *enfant terrible* of the Commission was the annual series of Audit Commission profiles. Each authority received its own profile, the main purpose of which is to compare the authority's spending per head of population with the average for a group of authorities having similar demographic and social characteristics. Authorities were grouped in accordance with a classification known as the Shaw classification and each group was referred to as an 'audit family'. For services where more appropriate client numbers than total population are readily available, e.g. school pupils in the education service, these are used. Differences in unit spending from the family average are converted into cash variances for further effect. This system has now been superseded by the annual publication of performance indicators (*see* below).

The Audit Commission has made a considerable impact on local government during its relatively short life span. Some might argue that it has done more harm than good by making unjustified claims on the basis of superficial investigation and analysis. However, it has to be accepted that the work of the Commission has done much to set local authority members and officers thinking along the right lines, i.e. about economy, efficiency and effectiveness or – in a word – about management.

2 Commercial

2.1 Project appraisal

Project appraisal is very much a corporate technique and the CFO is only one of many participants, but he or she will invariably draw together the results of the appraisal. Strictly speaking, no commitment to incur additional resources in the future should be approved by a local authority without being accompanied by a project appraisal. Such a criterion would cover the entire capital programme. In some local authorities, this is the position. In most, however, only the most complex, political or expensive projects are appraised fully.

A project appraisal should cover, amongst others, the following factors:

- objective of project;
- method of achieving objective;
- alternative methods of achievement and why these have been discarded;
- resource costs:
  - financial – capital and revenue (with revenue shown over several forward years);
  - staffing requirements and likely availability;
  - land needs and availability;

- effects on IT and systems, central accommodation and other consequences;

■ benefits:

  - financial, including rates of return if possible;

  - subjective, preferably presented in some form of tabular format;

■ priority index (difficult to achieve, but possible with a corporate approach);

■ other relevant points, such as relationship with other services/outside bodies, etc.

Good project appraisals are difficult to accomplish. They are time consuming to construct and require intelligent and experienced analytical people to prepare them. Over and above the analyst's recommendations, there is a need for very senior or chief officer input and involvement of members, particularly in relation to benefits and a priority index. This latter criterion may seem to be slightly cosmetic, but given that the public sector is always in the situation of having scarce resources, any help in determining priorities must be welcome.

Cost/benefit analysis has had a checkered career over the years but without the comprehensive and objective approach associated with that technique, project appraisal would be no more than an arithmetical exercise. Decision-makers need the kind of help which cost/benefit analysis can give and it is for the corporate staff to provide it, with the CFO playing a major part.

We are conscious that these paragraphs only touch the surface of project appraisal and have not discussed the techniques involved. These, however, could easily form the substance of another book – which we are not volunteering to write.

2.2 Business planning and support

The growth of business planning and support is a direct result of the Local Government Act 1988 which led to the immediate extension of CCT to the catering, refuse collection, vehicle maintenance, grounds maintenance and cleaning activities of local authorities.

In the wake of this legislation those local authorities wishing to give the relevant in-house staff the chance to compete have established DSOs. As potential contractors, DSOs have had to be given a separate management structure from that of the local authority (the client). The immediate role of the business support teams has been to provide dedicated support and advice to the DSOs, particularly in the following areas:

- **business planning** – forecasting, modelling, financial projections, pricing, cash flow, investment;

- **financial advice** – development of management information and accounting systems, tender evaluation, preparation of tender bids, review of overheads, advice to DSO board;

- **financial monitoring/control** – budgetary control, inflation monitoring, income monitoring, performance review;

- **preparation of final accounts** – closing timetable, trading accounts and flow of funds statements, rates of return, financial statistics, liaison with external auditor.

This list is by no means exhaustive but it gives a fair indication of the expertise which DSO managers must be able to call on if they are to operate successfully. Clearly this expertise must be independent of the financial support provided for the local authority as client.

This account emphasises the financial aspects of business planning and support. There is also a requirement for non-financial support, particularly in relation to personnel, property and legal matters. Although in many authorities the business support team is located in the CFO's department, it could equally be sited in a different department or in a separate location altogether, as it is funded by the DSOs and ultimately accountable to the DSO Board.

2.3 Asset management

Asset management is a corporate function with inputs from:

- establishments;

- service departments; and

- specialist departments (e.g. property, personnel, finance, legal).

The degree of specialisation depends upon the nature of the asset, which can be land and buildings, equipment, people (staff), roads, etc. For convenience, we are limiting this section on asset management to the management of land and buildings and the CFO's role in that process.

The basis of any asset management system is appropriate information, and many local authorities now have computerised databases for property which have the capacity of handling common data for a variety of purposes. Corporate access is allowed and the systems can be designed on a modular basis which enhances flexibility. Such systems would include property information, referenced on a geographic basis, with the following details:

- address and type of property;

- custodian(s);

- tenure of land and key review dates;

- maintenance information;

- building areas – usage and spare capacity;

- cleaning areas;

- details of fixtures and fittings and movable equipment, if appropriate;

- rent payment, if relevant.

It is clear from this list that property management is primarily concerned with physical characteristics and there is a minimum of financial information. What is increasingly required is information on the economic cost of the property so that assessments can be made from time to time at a macro level on the viability of the property.

CFOs in the past have not kept financial asset records on this basis. Financial information relating to a property has been based purely on how that property was financed. This could be by:

- borrowing by external loan, which has to be repaid;

- borrowing from internal capital funds, which need not be repaid;

- renting;

- leasing – finance or operational;

- proceeds of capital receipts;

- a one-off contribution from the revenue budget.

This information is irrelevant for the purposes of property management and a new voluntary code of practice on capital accounting has now been introduced (*see* Appendix C). One of the objectives of this new approach is to look at each type of asset and assess a proper charge for its usage. This charge should appear in service financial statements, management accounts and individual property records. This will certainly raise the profile of asset management in the second half of the 1990s, which can be no bad thing.

2.4 Value for money

Value for money or is now familiar enough to most local authority managers to render a detailed explanation of the concept unnecessary. Internal audit staff within the CFO's department should for some time have been shifting the emphasis of their activities from regularity audit to VFM work. External auditors will certainly have been doing so, given the considerable effort that the Audit Commission has put into their VFM studies.

It is probable that every local authority has by now carried out its own VFM initiatives either at the corporate or the service level. Special multi-disciplinary teams may have been established to identify areas suitable for VFM review and either to undertake VFM studies or to commission other colleagues or outside consultants to do so. Reports will have been prepared, perhaps containing impressive lists of potential savings. And then. . .?

The purpose of this seemingly disparaging résumé is not to cast doubt on the merits of VFM initiatives but to emphasise strongly that they are only of lasting value if their recommendations are implemented thoroughly and kept under review. If VFM studies are to be carried out and implemented successfully a number of requirements must be met:

- Senior managers from the service areas to be studied must be part of the VFM team.

- Specialist advice must be available either within the team or from outside to assist in drawing up the terms of reference for the study.

- The leader of the VFM team must be of sufficient status to deal on equal terms with any chief officer affected by the study.

- Studies should be limited to identifying more efficient and economic ways of providing the existing service. It may become evident during a study that the best solution is to change the nature or level or service provided. At this point the exercise becomes one of policy review rather than VFM and it is vital to recognise when this occurs.

Considerations of this sort have tended to encourage a corporate approach to VFM work. Unfortunately, although corporate studies are often more effective in identifying savings, they are also more difficult to implement than studies which are internal to particular services. Managers affected by but not involved in corporate VFM studies may well not identify with the recommendations and may have little incentive to implement them, particularly if it is decided to use any savings that are realised for corporate purposes. We would certainly not argue that all VFM savings should be retained locally. However, an agreed division of savings may be an effective compromise in those authorities where the corporate ethos is not sufficient to guarantee the whole-hearted commitment of service managers to the corporate good.

Of course, for VFM work to be effective in the long term it must become routine management function. There is increasing recognition of this and corporate VFM teams are beginning to give way to:

- service-level VFM programmes, designed to cover all activities over a period of three to five years;

- centrally imposed targets for VFM savings, e.g. 0.5 per cent of the net revenue budget for each service;

- performance review – a much broader exercise of which VFM is an integral part.

2.5 Investment management

Investment management is very much a function of the CFO – often personally. London boroughs, county councils and a lead district in each metropolitan area have the task of investing the local authority superannuation fund for their areas. This fund pays out pensions to retired administrative staff and manual workers. It does not cover teachers, police or uniformed fire service employees. The sums involved are very large. Large counties and the lead metropolitan districts account for thousands of millions of pounds and are significant institutional investors.

Despite a growing body of regulations and guidelines on investment management, there is considerable discretion in this area. However, local authorities must take proper advice and act with reasonable care, skill and caution. Some of the other investment principles which must be followed include:

- the pursuit of long-term benefits in order to pay pensions well into the twenty-first century;

- discouraging short-term 'trading'. Funds are exempt from tax and too much trading could affect this status;

- management must be seen to be professional, in terms of both the people involved and the degree to which this is a full-time continuous role;

- investments should be prudent. Investing a significant proportion of the fund in oil exploration or gold prospecting would not be considered prudent;

- investments should be reasonably diverse. Excessive holdings in particular companies or countries or sectors in the market may be outside the regulations.

There are of course political stances which the trustees, a small group of councillors usually advised by specialists, might decide to take. A refusal to invest in South Africa is a historical example. It is unlikely, however, that any stance like this has ever been of sufficient significance to affect the long-term performance of funds. Of growing significance, however, is the role which institutional investors, including pension funds, play as major shareholders of companies in the conduct of those companies. A recent example was the decision in 1995 by many local authority pension funds which held shares in British Gas to vote against large pay rises for senior executives of that company.

Investment management can take a variety of forms and since the 'Big Bang' in 1986, when the organisation of stock market operations was revolutionised, the variety has grown significantly. Some current options include:

- a single in-house manager;

- as above, plus an external manager with 50 per cent of the fund 'in competition';

- two or more different types of manager 'in competition';

- specialist external managers for, say:
  - gilt-edged securities;
  - UK equities;
  - USA;
  - Japan;
  - Europe;
  - other countries;
  - property;
  - temporary cash investment;

- a specialist asset allocation manager (i.e. one who will determine the proportion of the fund to invest in the categories listed above);

- indexation of all or part of the fund to track a selected investment index (with the intention of matching the growth or otherwise of the selected market as a whole).

The whole business is fascinating and, of course, very important financially. Actuaries now value the superannuation fund every three years and the employers' contribution is determined by that valuation. If an authority out-performs the 'average' by 1 per cent, that may be worth £1 or 2 million per year to the fund. Fund administrators now publish one-year, five-year and ten-year performance figures and these will only serve to accentuate interest in the relative performance of different kinds of fund management and the different financial institutions involved.

3 Information/advice

3.1 Financial advice

The CFO and his or her staff act as financial advisers to three different client groups:

- elected members;

- senior managers in other departments;

- other managers and all staff in outside establishments and service departments.

In terms of staff hours required the last of these represents the greatest commitment. It is also vital to the smooth running of the authority that advice at this level is readily available, sound and consistent. As the pressure on service providers continues to mount, it is increasingly important for the CFO to have sufficient suitably qualified and experienced staff to meet this need. Not surprisingly such staff are becoming increasingly difficult to recruit and retain.

The challenges in providing financial advice to the other client groups are somewhat different. The most important issue is the need for financial advice to be given as or on behalf of:

- the responsible financial officer with a statutory corporate duty to ensure 'the proper administration of [the authority's] financial affairs'; and

- a professional adviser whose fees are paid by a client service or group of services and who should therefore treat the clients' interests as paramount.

There is here a potential conflict between the interests of a particular client service and the corporate interest, and this often poses a dilemma for the CFO or his/her representative in giving advice. Should advice be 'limiting' so as to ensure probity and protect the corporate interest or should it be 'enabling' so as to promote a particular service activity?

It may be argued, with justification, that if the appropriate corporate ethos is well established and if there is a proper corporate strategy, this dilemma should not arise. In practice, neither condition is likely to be fully satisfied. This problem has become particularly evident in those authorities which have restructured the CFO's department into service-based, rather than functional, divisions. The responsibility of the divisional manager to his or her client department is much clearer now than was the case previously. This link will be further reinforced when SLAs are in place. This emphasises once more the need for an influential core within the CFO's department which has no vested service interest.

3.2 Management information

This topic has been covered at length in Chapter 5 and also features in other chapters. It therefore requires no further exposition at this stage.

3.3 Financial training

A recurring theme of this book is the need for adequate financial training if decentralisation of financial management during the 1990s is to strengthen rather than weaken local government. This training need covers a very wide range of people. The introduction of LMS generated an urgent demand in the average LEA to train around 3000 school governors, 200 head teachers, and a similar number of bursars, clerical staff in schools and centrally based support staff. This was a massive commitment which was clearly beyond the resources of the CFO's department. It could only be met by a combination of:

- formal training by outside trainers, dedicated LMS staff and CFO staff;
- cascade training – for example, having been given formal training, head teachers acted as trainers for their governors and senior staff;
- training packages, including videos;
- regular meetings and personal visits;
- leaflets, circulars and newsheets;
- guidance manuals.

The lessons learned from this exercise should enable LEAs to utilise limited resources to provide more and better financial training in the long term.

However, there is no escaping the fact that effective training, whether in-house or not, takes time and/or money. Either way it must be given high priority and proper resources.

3.4 Performance review

Performance review is becoming an essential element of financial management in the 1990s. It is required to:

- demonstrate that local authorities are achieving their objectives effectively, efficiently and economically;

- indicate areas of responsibility which are in need of review;

- clarify managerial responsibilities within local authorities and assess how well they are being achieved.

One of the longstanding obstacles to the development of performance review has already been referred to. This is the difficulty of identifying quantifiable output measures for many local authority services. Significant progress has recently been made in this area, not so much through the invention of novel performance indicators but rather by sustained efforts, particularly on the part of CIPFA and the Audit Commission, to consolidate and structure the mass of information which is available to fuel the performance review process.

Several categories of performance measure are now available, including:

- **Unit costs** Although this is an input measure it can be useful in assessing performance if there is a standard or average with which to compare, e.g. cost per primary school pupil;

- **Output indicators** These are service volumes possibly expressed per unit of resource input, e.g. numbers of local searches per staff day, or as a ratio of the potential demand, e.g. library service members per 1000 population.

- **Utilisation rates** These show the percentage of full capacity at which a service is operating, e.g. occupancy percentage of an elderly persons' home.

- **Service times** These are the average time taken to perform a particular activity or service, e.g. the time taken to process a mandatory student award application.

Although none of these indicators provides a thorough indication of output or effectiveness, each enables useful comparisons to be made:

- over time; or

- between authorities; or

- against regional, class of authority or national averages or standards.

Particular care should be taken over inter-authority comparisons because there may be inconsistencies in the way that the relevant statistics have been measured, analysed and presented. The impact of Audit Commission profile information has to some extent been undermined by the ease with which major variances from the audit family average can be attributed to inconsistencies and anomalies.

The spring of 1995 saw a new Government-backed venture linked with the Citizens Charter, namely the publication by the Audit Commission of a range of performance indicators for all local authorities. The indicators were based on actual spending and service statistics for the 1993/94 financial year. They included:

- expenditure per school pupil (primary and secondary);

- proportion of children on child protection register;

- percentage of Council tax collected;

- total expenditure per head of population.

The publication of performance indicators for the 1994/95 financial year has made it possible to assess the year-on-year change in performance of individual authorities and classes of authority, as well as making inter-authority comparisons.

It must be said that, so far, the impact of published performance indicators has been somewhat muted. There are a number of obvious reasons for this, such as:

- the traditional indifference of the general public to detailed statistical information, particularly about local government;

- the retrospective nature of the information (it appeared a full year after the end of the period to which it related);

- the limited scope of the published information, which is largely determined by the statistical database;

- the extent to which 'experts' were able to blame anomalies and exceptional circumstances for below-average performance.

The above reference to the Citizens Charter merits a few additional comments on what was the first distinct policy initiative by the present Prime Minister. As explained in the 1991 White Paper, the Citizens Charter initiative is an agenda for the subsequent development of charters covering a wide range of public services. The stated objectives of the initiative are to:

- raise quality;
- increase choice;
- secure better value for money;
- extend accountability.

The possible mechanisms for achieving these aims were identified as:

- competition, privatisation and contracting out;
- performance-related pay;
- independent inspectorates;
- published performance targets and information on standards;
- proper procedures for making complaints and seeking redress.

This is not the place for a lengthy critique of the Citizens Charter. It has certainly been taken up by some authorities as an element of their marketing and public relations strategy. However, we do not sense that it has had much influence so far on the underlying quality of local services. Performance targets and charter promises inevitably focus on what can be measured, which is not always of prime importance. In addition, we feel that the Citizens Charter is part of a culture in which everyone is encouraged to regard themselves as a consumer, rather than as a citizen or a member of the community. An obvious manifestation of this is an increased tendency on the part of the general public to complain about decisions and actions taken by local authorities. This would be perfectly healthy if these decisions and actions were based on local discretion and reasonable access to resources. To the extent that they are based on central Government prescription and inadequate funding, the present trends are unhelpful.

On a more positive note another new aspect of performance review is now being promoted, particularly in relation to school improvement. This technique is known as 'benchmarking' and it involves comparing chosen indicators for a particular school, e.g. the proportion of the budget spent on administrative staff, with the corresponding averages for all schools in the area and also perhaps with regional or national average figures. It is important to recognise that benchmarking simply tells the school where it is in relation to others; it does not provide a detailed view of how to improve. In addition, there is a risk that a slavish adherence to benchmarking could stifle innovation, by creating pressure for standardisation. However, it is considered that, if sensibly employed, benchmarking may pose relevant questions and is therefore a useful practical technique of performance review.

Footnote

Efforts, particularly by CIPFA, to improve the scope and comparability of performance indicators, particularly in sensitive areas such as support services, are an important element in the development of performance review. The key role which CIPFA and many individual local authorities play in compiling and publishing detailed service statistics should be recognised and sustained. Unfortunately, this activity is increasingly under threat because of financial restrictions. It would indeed be ironic if performance review were to be undermined by a growing inability on the part of local authorities to complete the statistical returns on which performance indicators must be based. This could happen if the quest for economy goes too far!

9

Progress in decentralising financial management

KEY POINTS

- During the 1990s progress in decentralising financial management has been patchy.

- Because of financial constraints, CCT, Local Government Review and loss of local authority functions, there has been more emphasis on developments which reduce costs than on initiatives to improve effectiveness.

- Service level agreements (SLAs) between the CFO's department and service departments or individual establishments have become common during the 1990s.

- SLAs make explicit the levels and standards of service to be provided by the CFO's department in respect of each function covered by the agreements; they also set out the associated charges.

- SLAs may be associated with minimum standards determined by the CFO to fulfil his or her statutory responsibility.

- SLAs provide a basis for decentralisation in the future, as well as for more radical measures, including competition for certain financial management and IT functions.

- SLAs and other initiatives have helped to bring a greater service focus into the operation of the CFO's department.

Introduction

In this chapter we shall review the development of financial management during the 1990s, particularly with regard to decentralisation of financial management functions. In doing so we shall introduce the concept of SLAs and discuss the role they have played in this process.

Decentralisation in practice

There is a saying that 'It is better to travel hopefully than to arrive'. In terms of the decentralisation of financial management functions, we sense that very few, if any, have arrived. In practice, change has tended to involve fragmentation, rather than decentralisation. In particular, there has been some externalisation of certain financial management and IT functions, achieved in the main by contracting out, establishing arm's length companies or management buy-outs. Where it has occurred, this fragmentation of the traditional CFO's department has certainly had a profound impact on the CFO and his/her staff, some of whom now have a new private sector employer and, possibly, different terms and conditions of service. Some staff may even have been transferred to other locations; others, of course, may have retired or been made redundant. Within the CFO's department, the remaining non-core financial management functions may now be organised into semi-autonomous business units, leaving a core finance division organised along the lines set out in Chapter 2.

Externalisation of financial management functions is almost certain to have some repercussions on service managers but, in theory, these should be beneficial or, at worst, neutral. The important point is that these initiatives are unlikely to achieve any greater degree of 'total management at the point of service delivery' than was the case before.

It must be said that in most local authorities the mid-point of the 1990s has been reached with the traditional functional structure of the CFO's department largely intact. There may have been some limited refinements such as a clearer separation between core and non-core financial management functions, more flexible financial regulations, particularly in terms of budget virements and year-end carry forwards, improved financial management information and service level agreements (*see* below). However, there are still many similarities with the structure and organisation which existed before 1990.

This obviously raises the possibility that decentralisation, as a model for the future, is inherently wrong or flawed in some way. We reject this suggestion, partly out of stubbornness, but also because we believe that, despite the statutory pressures of CCT and LMS, the climate during the first half of the 1990s has been profoundly hostile to developments which, like decentralisation, have a long lead time, involve transitional costs and promote service effectiveness rather than resource savings.

The challenges of the 1990s

A shortage of money will naturally stimulate activity to reduce costs in the short term. It does not encourage a strategy which promotes long-term improvements in efficiency and effectiveness, and which may lead to higher costs in the short term. No one has enough money and it is all too easy to use this as an excuse for many of the ills which currently beset local government. The problem for local authorities has been that, not only have they had to operate within a tight financial framework during the 1990s, but also the surrounding environment has been unstable and fraught with uncertainty.

Instability and uncertainty have been created by further massive upheaval in the system of local government finance, with the introduction of the community charge or poll tax being followed almost immediately by its 'overthrow' and the introduction of the Council tax (see Appendix B). The Local Government Review has since claimed centre stage and, after much coming and going, has led ultimately to the creation of 46 new unitary authorities. The situation has been made even more volatile by further transfers of functions into and out of the local authority sector. 'Care in the community' has brought the responsibility for many mentally ill and mentally handicapped people into local government from the Health Service. The process has had major social, professional, managerial and financial repercussions. On the other hand, LEAs have lost further education colleges and the responsibility for school inspection to non-elected QUANGOs.

There has been another less dramatic but equally profound development in recent years, namely the extension of the 'bidding culture' in local government. Although most local authority functions are supported by a general grant, known as revenue support grant, some have traditionally been funded by means of specific or supplementary grants. Linking Government grant funding to a particular activity is an effective way of ensuring that every authority carries out the activity in the manner and at the level desired by Government. A good example is teacher training, which is supported by a range of specific grants known as GEST (Grants for Education Support and Training). Such grants may also be appropriate where not every authority is involved in a particular activity. Therefore National Parks Supplementary Grant is only paid to those authorities in whose areas there are designated National Parks, and only authorities with substantial ethnic minority communities are eligible for a Section 11 Grant. There is another category of grants associated with functions, including housing benefit and mandatory student awards, where national regulations apply and the function of local government is that of the administering authority. Last but not least the Police Grant and the Transport Supplementary Grant apply to services of national importance, where a significant measure of central Government control is deemed appropriate.

Although there has always been an element of bidding within the framework of some specific grants, the grant levels in most cases are determined by formula, negotiation, actual expenditure or some combination of these. Bidding has come to the fore quite recently, partly because grant rationing has been found to be a useful way of containing public expenditure and also because of the Government's wish to introduce competition and private sector involvement into local authority spending programmes, particularly urban regeneration projects involving Labour-controlled inner-city authorities. Over time the network of grants associated with economic and social regeneration has become so complicated and costly that drastic rationalisation has been attempted, and there is now a single bidding framework known as the single regeneration budget (SRB).

There is a third important ingredient of the emergent bidding culture, namely the European Union (EU). This is certainly not the place to explore the intricacies of EU finance, but certain EU structural funds, particularly the European Regional Development Fund (ERDF) and the European Social Fund (ESF), are now a source of substantial grant support to local authorities in certain areas of the United Kingdom. It will come as no surprise to learn that the process for allocating EU grants is totally inexplicable, but preparing bids is certainly an integral part of it! The most recent and best known element of the bidding culture is the National Lottery, which is set to become the principal, if not the only, source of grant funding for projects involving sports, the arts and national heritage.

It would be unfair to argue that the growth in competitive bidding to finance local authority activities has been, of itself, harmful to financial management decentralisation. Indeed, the bidding culture requires the sort of multi-disciplinary project approach which ought to be wholly compatible with a decentralised framework. However, the bidding procedures associated with

SRB and EU grants are complex, ill-defined, extremely time consuming and, of course, not guaranteed to achieve success. In addition, the large scale and complexity of these national and European funding mechanisms make them especially vulnerable to political interference. Whatever its intrinsic merits, the competitive bidding regime has so far been cumbersome and inefficient.

The enabling authority

As well as coping with service pressures, financial constraints and novel funding mechanisms, local government has spent the first half of the 1990s coming to terms with the combined effect of CCT, Local Government Review, the Citizens Charter and the Government's efforts to marginalise the local authority role in education and housing. This process of self-analysis led to an extension of the purchaser/provider split, as described in Chapter 4, towards the concept of the enabling authority. At the extreme, the enabling authority is characterised by a single Council meeting each year at which the contracts are let for all the services for which the authority is responsible. The authority does not employ any service providers, but does employ a relatively small but multi-skilled group of people who prepare service specifications, manage the tendering and evaluation processes and monitor performance once the contracts have been let. This is a dramatic extension of the approach put forward in Chapter 2 for financial management functions, but now applied to the entire local authority.

The idea of the enabling authority is not one that is immediately appealing to those directly involved in local government – elected members, staff or trade unions – since, for the most part, they appear to become insignificant or irrelevant. At the present time, therefore, very few authorities have advanced far down this track. However, the philosophy of 'enabling' is supported to varying degrees by all three main political parties, and cannot be ignored in current management thinking.

Service levels and costs

If there is one common strand in the complex and confusing scenario described so far in this book, it is the need for a clearer picture within local authorities of service levels and costs. In order to cope effectively with LMS, CCT, Charter initiatives, published performance indicators, competitive bidding and all the rest, it is vital to have detailed information about all the activities in which the local authority is involved, in terms of quantity, quality and cost. Only if this information is available can sensible judgements be made about securing effective and efficient services for the community.

This fundamental requirement affects the CFO and his/her staff in a number of ways. In the first place, the CFO obviously has a key role in developing accurate and detailed information on costs, particularly if he/she also has corporate responsibility for IT. Equally important, however, is the requirement for the CFO to draw up service specifications and cost statements for all the financial management functions which come under his/her control. When this has been done, but not before, sensible decisions can be made about delegating or decentralising financial management functions.

Once detailed information on service levels and costs is available the next question is who has responsibility for the relevant budgets. In a traditional centralised system, the CFO controls the budgets for most, if not all, financial management functions, and the relevant staff are based in the CFO's department. In order to meet the Code of Practice on Local Authority Accounting (*see* Chapter 2) which requires most overhead costs to be charged to front-line services, the non-core costs of the CFO's department are allocated or apportioned to other service departments and trading accounts. Our convention here is that 'allocation' implies that the charge is based on actual cost or usage, whereas 'apportionment' implies a fixed or formula distribution of costs which is only loosely related to usage. For example, if payroll costs for the year are shared out between departments according to the number of payroll records or actual payments processed in that year, this would qualify as an allocation. If the costs were shared out on the basis of overall staff numbers or service budgets, we would consider this an apportionment.

The totality of local authority overhead costs has various titles, a traditional one being 'central establishment charges'. As has already been pointed out there are valid reasons why these overhead costs, which are now more commonly referred to as support service costs, are higher than in the private sector. In addition, the Local Authority Accounting Code of Practice allows for some of these costs to be accounted for separately, e.g. service strategy and regulation, democratic representation. The remainder are charged to services on some basis or other and it is not surprising that, in an era of financial constraint and competitive pressures, elected members and service managers are keen to ensure that:

- these charges represent as small a proportion as possible of overall service costs; and

- service departments and trading services can influence the level and quality of the associated support services.

It is then a fairly small but important step to the point where all service managers begin to view their relationship with support service departments, including the CFO's department, in the same way as DSO managers (*see* Chapter 4). Suggestions may even come forward that the budgets for some or all of the financial management functions carried out by the CFO's staff should be devolved to the users of those services. In our view this is the stage that many local authorities have reached at the mid-point of the 1990s, although we recognise and applaud those pioneering authorities who are well beyond this point. Our next task is to describe one of the mechanisms that has been crucial in supporting this changing relationship, namely the SLA.

Service level agreements

Service level agreements for financial management functions recognise that, in theory, there are three distinct choices facing the service manager who requires financial support, namely:

- to buy the relevant services from the CFO;

- to buy them from an external accountancy, financial services or banking concern;

- to provide them in-house, i.e. within the service department or establishment.

Clearly the above options are not mutually exclusive; a combination of all three approaches might provide the best solution for the service manager.

How does the service manager decide what to do? More specifically, what information will need to be available to allow a sensible decision to be made? In our view the manager needs to know, for each option:

- the scope and quality of service available in respect of each financial management function;

- the associated costs.

In the traditional local authority situation, the CFO was the provider of most non-core financial services, particularly the basic exchequer functions of payroll, creditors and income. The detailed specification of the services being provided was well known to the CFO's staff but not to anyone outside the CFO's department. Information on costs was almost certainly confined to an annual recharge to each department or establishment for central support services, within which it might or might not be possible to identify the charge for financial services.

The above scenario hardly provides the service manager with a sound basis for exercising the choice of options described earlier. Service level agreements between the CFO's department and service departments or establishments provide a way forward by bringing together and making explicit the standards of and charges for services being provided. They also, of course, provide a vehicle for the service manager to negotiate the non-core financial services available from the CFO.

The structure and content of SLAs is described in Appendix D. The practical detail of SLAs should not obscure the key aspects of the new relationship, which are:

- the existence of a written agreement;

- a degree of flexibility for the customer as well as the CFO;

- accountability;

- an agreed charging structure;

- a mechanism for arbitration and dealing with poor performance.

The requirement to work to a written agreement is a cultural revolution for many finance departments, and other central departments as well, for SLAs are applicable to all. The days of central establishment recharges are numbered. Chief financial officers now have to agree with their customers in advance exactly what service they want and how much it will cost. Subject to minimum standards determined by the CFO, the customer or the service manager is free to vary his or her detailed requirements. These might involve totally new services, or simply a more or less detailed check than the CFO's staff have previously carried out on certain transactions. The service manager has to pay for any enhanced requirement. Once an agreement has been made, the service manager knows his or her financial commitment for the period ahead, unless variations are agreed in the interim.

The agreement can be varied, particularly to allow for:

- pay and prices, although the concept of cash limits may mean that many agreements are at out-turn prices;

- changes in service level at the behest of the service manager, rather than the CFO;

- unplanned audit work as the result of suspicion of irregularities, etc.;

- matters outside the direct control of either party to the agreement (e.g. industrial action).

At the end of the financial year, the service manager should be charged in accordance with the SLA together with any agreed variations. If the specified quantity of work has not been achieved (e.g. the audit programme has not been fulfilled) then the overall charge should be less. If the quality of work is below specification in the view of the service manager, then a lower charge may be appropriate but the scale of reduction may be difficult to determine.

If the CFO has not fulfilled his or her contract with a service manager, there are four possible explanations:

- resources within CFO's department were switched during the year to undertake work for another service manager;

- the CFO's resources were insufficient because of staff vacancies;

- the amount of work involved was underestimated;

- the CFO's staff were less productive than planned, due to poor quality, lack of training, excessive turnover, etc.

In the first two cases, the CFO may be able to agree a reduced charge while still balancing his books, either because another service manager can be charged more or because vacancies have reduced costs. In the latter two examples however, the CFO is likely to incur a deficit in his or her trading account unless a contingency for this eventuality has been built into charges. The CFO's trading account is debited with all the costs of the CFO's department and is credited with the charges contained in all the SLAs involving the CFO's department, adjusted for agreed variations. The bottom line will be a surplus or a deficit. This will provide the ultimate accountability on the performance of the CFO and his or her staff.

The way charges are structured is critical to the success or otherwise of SLAs. It has to be remembered that the CFO has only a limited number of customers. Private financial advisers/operators have numerous customers and consequently tend to have reasonably simple charging structures, e.g. £X per hour for different levels of staff or £Y per unit processed. Usually they will only give a firm price if the work involved is of predictable and limited duration.

By contrast, CFOs can operate between two basic extremes in structuring charges. At one extreme everything could be on a marginal cost basis – £X per hour or y pence per unit. Alternatively there could be a fixed price for the whole package, irrespective of the quantity of input. In practice there is likely to be a two-part tariff, with a fixed or standard charge and a variable or unit charge, just as there is in gas, electricity and telephone charges. The CFO has to decide what proportion of his/her overall costs come into the fixed category in the short to medium term and what is clearly marginal and can be adjusted quickly if the need arises.

A good example of this can be seen in relation to the payment of creditors. Let us assume that the costs of the payments function are as set out in Table 9.1.

Table 9.1

	£ per annum	£ per annum
Financial systems	25 000	
Section head	15 000	
Accommodation	5 000	45 000
Five payments staff		45 000
Gross annual cost		90 000

Let us also assume that there are expected to be 90 000 invoices processed per annum. The estimated average processing cost is £1 per invoice. The CFO could say to the service manager that the cost of the service will be £1 per invoice processed. If in the event only 72 000 invoices are processed, then income to the CFO will be only £72 000. However, in the short term the CFO can only save the salary of one member of the payments staff as each member can process 18 000 invoices annually. This will lead to a net loss of £9000. Alternatively, if the CFO charges a fixed fee of £45 000 and 50 pence per invoice processed, then income to the CFO will be £81 000, a reduction of only £9000. This is equal to the potential saving in staff costs. It can be seen therefore that the way charges are structured is very important to the viability of the CFO's trading account.

An SLA must deal with the questions of how and by whom disputes arising about the quality of service are resolved. In financial circles we all have our own ideas about the quality of consultants' reports and the work of external auditors. Some are excellent, others we believe are less than average. Judgements are qualitative and difficult to define. Standards to measure against are difficult to find. Performance standards should be contained in SLAs wherever possible. Examples are:

- to pay creditors correctly within X days of the receipt of the invoice;

- to collect at least 99 per cent of all income within X weeks of receiving an account;

- to pay at least 99.5 per cent of employees correctly on the due date.

Penalties can be included in the SLA when performance is outside the agreed parameters. This may be easier said than done because in a complex situation with different departments/establishments participating in a single transaction, it is not easy to apportion blame. Nevertheless if true accountability is to be achieved, solutions must be found.

What is even more difficult to define is how to monitor the quality of financial advice, audit work, VFM reports and the general provision of financial information. Moreover, with the greatest of respect to legal colleagues, we are not sure that they could adjudicate on such matters. If serious arguments develop in these areas, there must be a very basic doubt about the viability of future relationships. In these circumstances a useful mediator could be the external auditor, although he or she would possibly disagree!

A framework for support services

If properly applied, SLAs for financial services bring a much higher level of clarity and accountability into the relationship between the CFO and the service manager. However, in order for SLAs to be wholly effective, they must operate within a clear and well understood corporate framework, such as the one outlined in Appendix D. This framework must be able to accommodate all support services, including those which are not covered by SLAs. Experience during the first half of the 1990s has shown that the SLA model is not yet appropriate for all local authority support services, and this may be the case indefinitely. A framework which allows for this, and makes clear the status of all support services, provides the soundest possible basis on which to plan future developments, whether or not decentralisation is on the agenda. The key requirements of any such framework are that it must:

- require a clear written specification for every support service;

- be possible to identify where the budget responsibility for each support service lies;

- ensure that the charging arrangements for each support service are clearly identified and are compatible with the budget responsibility;

- allow appropriate minimum requirements to be specified for each support service.

It will be noted that, even where SLAs are not in force, there should still be a written statement of the services which are to be provided. Such documents have become known as 'service level statements'.

The third requirement is very important. It is of little benefit to have a sophisticated charging mechanism on paper, which encourages a service department to manage its consumption of a particular support service, if the relevant portion of the support service budget is outside the control of the service department.

The final requirement is absolutely crucial for the CFO because, although not the only potential supplier of some financial services, he/she alone must fulfil the statutory responsibilities set out in Chapter 2, which cover economy and probity, as well as effectiveness and efficiency. Minimum requirements might cover such issues as:

- the expertise and viability of alternative suppliers;

- any statutory requirements which must be met in respect of the service concerned;

- information which the CFO requires from the service provider to fulfil his/her responsibilities.

Competition for financial services

White-collar CCT raises the spectre that a wide range of financial management functions will soon be exposed to competition (*see* Chapter 4). It is therefore important that every local authority seeks to maximise effectiveness and efficiency in the provision of non-core financial management functions. The introduction of SLAs within a corporate framework for support services makes it possible to establish a situation where competition is sustainable in practice and clearly beneficial to the service manager.

For those financial management functions not affected by CCT it is only fair and reasonable that the CFO should be allowed sufficient time to prepare for competition. This suggests that the concept of SLAs should be allowed to work through from an experimental stage to a firm base for tendering. In those areas where SLAs are not yet in place, a suitable programme might be as follows:

- **Year 1** SLAs are produced for the first time – largely based on estimated figures of time spent on various functions with estimated allocations of cost to those functions. The budget remains under the direct control of the CFO but a shadow trading account is prepared.

- **Year 2**   SLAs are produced with more meaningful figures of service standards, volumes and costs. The budget for financial management functions should now be allocated to the service departments in accordance with the SLAs. Service managers are not allowed to vire any budgetary provision to other expenditure heads without the express approval of the CFO. The CFO's trading account is debited with actual costs and credited with the budget allocations after any agreed virements.

- **Year 3**   As for Year 2 but the service manager is allowed to retain all, or a proportion, of savings realised through the SLA, provided that minimum requirements are satisfied. The trading account is credited with the actual income due under the charges agreed in the SLA.

- **Year 4**   The service manager may be allowed to seek tenders from other providers of financial services and retain some or all of any consequential savings.

A four-year programme to extend competition for financial services might seem to be too long. However, there are various organisational changes which may become necessary during the process. In addition, we consider that in-house staff should be given a genuine opportunity of successfully competing for the work. A careful but determined approach is therefore recommended.

Lastly, we should briefly mention the types of competition that are emerging in this area. We do not have the research evidence to provide comprehensive advice on this! We shall simply note some of the alternatives of which we are aware.

One of the key decisions to be made would be how to package any contract(s). There is a wide range of options, from a single contract for all financial management functions to a series of separate contracts for each function. A further possibility would be a contract based on a series of establishments (on a geographical or service basis). There are several other permutations.

The competition which emerges could also take a variety of forms, such as:

- local or national firms of accountants for some or all of the work;

- various bureaux which specialise in exchequer work;

- banks or other financial institutions;

- computer companies for the provision of operations/development work and possibly other financial services;

- a management 'buy-out' which could be done through a separately created company, independent of the local authority.

A number of local authorities have already exposed a range of financial management functions to some sort of competition, although we do not have any information on their progress. The very fact that many local authorities have already embraced such major changes in the way they operate, and in the delivery of their central services, is both a tribute to their foresight and a reflection of their continued commitment to effective, efficient and economic local government in the future.

10
Towards the millennium

KEY POINTS

- The remainder of the 1990s will see a renewed emphasis on service effectiveness.

- Local authorities will increasingly work in partnership with other agencies, including locally managed schools, to secure high quality services for the community.

- Finance managers will be judged on their ability to support this process.

- The number of finance managers and staff based outside the CFO's department will continue to increase.

- It will become increasingly important to provide proper career development and promotion opportunities for finance staff based outside the CFO's department in order to attract and retain them.

- A coherent framework for local authority support services will provide a sound basis for making informed decisions about externalisation and decentralisation of financial management functions.

- Information technology and electronic communications will help to achieve effective, efficient and economic management of local authority services.

- Strategic planning and performance review will play a proper role in the development of local government.

Introduction

The objective of this concluding chapter is to speculate on the kind of financial management framework within local government which might emerge from the 1990s. Much depends on the relationship between central and local government during the second half of the decade. If the national political agenda continues to be dominated by:

- reducing the burden of public expenditure;

- reliance on free market mechanisms to determine public spending priorities;

- extending private sector involvement in public service provision;

- marginalising the role of local authorities;

there is every prospect that local authorities will continue to be pulled this way and that in attempting to interpret and implement a succession of conflicting national policies in the best interests of their local communities. The scope for sensible forward planning and managed change will remain very limited.

Hope springs eternal and we are determined to end on an optimistic note. Let us speculate, therefore, that there will soon be a more hospitable environment for local government, and that individual local authorities will be allowed once again to focus their energies on meeting local needs and priorities. This is not to suggest in any way that we can expect a return to the 'good old days' before capping, CCT and the Citizens Charter. Public expenditure control, competition and performance review will remain very much to the fore in the coming years, whatever the complexion of central government. Indeed, having faced up to the challenge of these constraints and pressures, it is important that local authorities continue to apply the new skills and techniques which have been so painfully acquired over recent years.

We consider that two aspects of the 'new agenda' will be particularly important. The first is, hopefully, a renewed emphasis on service effectiveness, where effectiveness is judged not only by factors which can be quantified, but by the extent to which local authority services meet the needs of their communities. The second is partnership, both between national and local government, and between local authorities and the communities they serve.

If this 'new agenda' is not to become rapidly discredited, it will need to be based on partnerships which are challenging and businesslike, not comfortable and informal. This imperative will apply to relationships within local authorities, as well as between local authorities and other agencies. Service level agreements, voluntary competition and even decentralisation will still have an important part to play.

In practical terms some of the key tasks of the CFO will, as before, be to:

- minimise the cost of financial management functions in order to allow the maximum resources to be deployed directly in additional service provision for the benefit of the community;

- ensure minimum financial standards are achieved;

- achieve the service quality and performance standards specified in the SLAs for financial management functions;

- deliver accurate, relevant, intelligible and timely financial information and advice to all levels of management.

We also envisage the CFO having to put added effort into specific areas of his/her responsibility, particularly the need to provide personal and career development for all those involved in financial management. This requirement is one we have not yet discussed, but it is obviously very important in ensuring the recruitment and retention of high-quality finance managers. It will become even more important and problematic if our expectations are fulfilled that finance managers increasingly are based in service departments and trading units, rather than in the CFO's department. This will be a key element in ensuring that financial management in the future has a clear service focus.

Management development

At present a major concern for every CFO is how he or she is going to staff the financial management functions in the next few years with people sufficiently well qualified and experienced to operate effectively, particularly in a service environment. Financial training in the public sector is generally of a high standard. The education and training arrangements of CIPFA are good, and accountants emerging from the system today are well equipped and therefore keenly sought after, particularly by the private sector. We therefore have a twofold task:

- to improve still further professional education and training arrangements, at both pre- and post-qualification stages;

- to retain finance staff in local authorities by offering suitable terms and conditions of employment, but also, and especially, job satisfaction and motivation.

It is not the role of this book to begin a detailed discussion of education and training arrangements and terms and conditions of service. What we are keen to do, however, is to put down a few markers as to how we feel these aspects should develop over the next few years. It is for others to further them, as CIPFA is already doing. Some matters requiring attention are:

- the need to eliminate the term 'accountant' and to replace it with 'finance manager'. The considerable emphasis on management training in the CIPFA professional syllabus is helpful;

- the need for service managers to allow and even encourage finance-based staff to participate in decisions about service provision;

- the importance of ensuring that the relevant finance manager is a member of the service management team;

- the need to encourage finance-based staff to apply for general management posts, including those of departmental service managers, and establishment heads.

We firmly believe that the image of accountants as narrow minded and unimaginative has finally to be dispelled. Training facilities to encourage the development of managerial skills should therefore continue to be a priority. Equally it is not a matter of training people just to provide the CFO's core function, but to cover the whole range of financial management functions. Ultimately the benchmark of success will be the extent to which financially trained personnel become service managers and heads of large establishments.

This is a vital issue because commitment and job satisfaction are major factors in retaining staff. Equally important, but often neglected or, worse still, despised, is the public service ethos which, after all, is why most of us entered local government. During the 1990s, from the poll tax to restructuring of local government, Council staff have time and again demonstrated their capacity to cope with even the most bizarre and unreasonable of demands. It is not performance-related pay that has sustained this effort, but the strong commitment of the staff concerned to the communities which they serve.

Towards the millennium

The following is a brief attempt to describe how the financial management of a large local authority might look in the year 2000 and then to discuss some of the resulting implications.

CFO's department

We outlined in Chapter 2 the core functions which, in our view, should always remain at the centre. They are basically concerned with standard setting, monitoring the quality of financial processing and co-ordinating financial information for the benefit of the local authority. The core also handles specialist services where it is uneconomical to decentralise and provides financial training in certain areas. The size of the core might be between 20 per cent and 30 per cent of the establishment of the traditional CFO's department. Any non-core financial management functions retained within the CFO's department will probably be managed as a separate business unit, which will operate on the basis of SLAs and full cost recovery.

The service department

It is not easy to be specific about the financial management role of the service department in the future. It may well provide support and guidance to individual establishments on routine procedures and also specific problems. It will certainly perform a monitoring role, and may carry out some internal audit work in its establishments. Recent developments in IT and electronic communications will make it possible for the exchequer functions of payroll, payment of creditors and collection of income to be carried out primarily by staff in individual establishments. If decentralisation proceeds along these lines, there will almost certainly be a need to transfer some of the CFO's staff to service departments. Although the overall number of support staff in service departments will probably decrease still further by the millennium, the number employed on financial management functions may remain reasonably stable, or possibly increase.

The establishment

Numbers of finance managers and support staff will continue to grow at this level. The local burden of providing financial information for the purposes of the establishment itself and also for the centre will increase and the volume of exchequer processing will be significantly greater. Exactly how this will be managed will depend upon several factors, including:

- **the size of the establishment** – the larger it is, the greater the possibility of attracting specialist staff and being able to afford them;

- **the location of the establishment** – if it is in an urban area it may be convenient to rely on the central service department for support. If it is in a rural location, there may be geographically based teams of specialists, including non-finance specialists, to serve all establishments in that area, irrespective of the type of service provision. The availability and cost of IT will be a key factor here.

Financial services DSOs

One option which some local authorities have embraced is a financial services organisation based on competitive principles. Under this scenario, the central provision of core functions would remain as we have already described. However, non-core financial services would be operated by a free-standing DSO. This organisation would not come under the control of service managers but would tender to provide financial services to them. It would encompass much of the existing work of the CFO's department and also significant parts of the financial administration at present within service departments. The CFO would, as before, be able to specify minimum financial standards.

This approach is similar to decentralisation in that it provides the service manager with choice in acquiring financial management services. However it is significantly different in structural and procedural terms. It represents the other end of the continuum within which there are a wide variety of operating arrangements for financial management functions, most of which will no doubt have been explored by the end of the 1990s.

Management information

One of the requirements we highlighted previously was that of delivering accurate, relevant, intelligible and timely information to all levels of management. Information will continue to be the key to effective management in the future, and the means of providing it will be a constant source of interest and concern. Most local authorities still have a large corporate financial database. This is an efficient way of storing data and producing information, but the format and content of reports may be less than ideal and even minor changes may well be difficult and expensive. Chapter 5 discussed the issues in greater detail.

The reason for stressing this matter again here is that unless useful and intelligible financial management information can be supplied on demand to managers, the service objectives of the establishment may be undermined. If the organisation of financial management functions is constrained by an inflexible financial information system, then it is unlikely that economies will result from reorganising the structure. Flexible information systems which can interact speedily with the corporate database and can also meet the control requirements of the core must be available. Some are already in place. By 2000 this should be much less of a problem, but there will undoubtedly be some more trials and tribulations on the way.

Performance review

Last but by no means least, we return belatedly to the issue of performance review. It is not wholly inappropriate to mention performance review at this late stage because its proper place is at the end of the cycle. We have already referred to performance review in Chapters 1, 3 and 8, but we feel it is important to reiterate that it will play a key role in future in achieving the effective, efficient and economic delivery of services.

As we have already pointed out, performance review in the local government context is a difficult process, not least because of the qualitative nature of many of the outputs and the general lack of profit motive. However, with the much sharper definition of objectives and standards of performance which will emerge as accountable management is defined at establishment level, there is a real opportunity to make significant inroads into performance measurement.

The development of performance review implies the existence of clear objectives and targets against which performance can be measured. This in turn requires that planning has taken place. In recent years, crisis management and opportunism have become so much a part of everyday life in local government that strategic planning has been marginalised and, to some extent, discredited. We see a revival of strategic planning, coupled with a renewed commitment to performance review, as key elements in the resurgence of local government as the millennium approaches. Let us hope that, with the benefit of our experience during the 1990s, we can make as positive a contribution to the twenty-first century as our colleagues and contemporaries have made to the twentieth!

Appendix A

Summary of financial management functions

1 Exchequer

1.1 Payroll	Salaries, wages, taxable expenses, superannuation contributions, income tax, national insurance, pay awards, increments, sick pay, maternity pay
1.2 Creditor payments	Invoices, non-taxable expenses, grants, awards
1.3 Council tax/ housing benefits	Council tax benefits, rent rebates/allowances
1.4 Income	Housing rents and other income (cash and credit)
1.5 Superannuation	Pension fund administration and payments to former employees
1.6 Non-domestic rate collection	
1.7 Council tax collection	
1.8 VAT administration	
1.9 Risk management and insurance	Claims, premiums and insurance fund

2 Co-ordination/control/accountability

2.1 Financial planning   Medium-term strategy
2.1.1 Annual revenue budget
2.1.2 Capital budgeting
2.2 Budgetary control   Monitoring, reporting and corrective action where necessary (revenue and capital)

2.3 Final accounts
2.4 Statutory reports and returns
2.4.1 Statutory financial returns
2.4.2 Annual report
2.4.3 Council tax notices
2.5 Grant claims and external funding
2.6 Cash flow management
2.7 Debt management   Including leasing and other financing arrangements

3 Audit/commercial/information and advice

3.1 Audit
3.1.1 Internal audit
3.1.2 External audit
3.2 Commercial
3.2.1 Project appraisal   Particularly capital programme
3.2.2 Business planning and support
3.2.3 Asset management
3.2.4 Value for money
3.2.5 Investment management   Particularly superannuation fund investments

3.3 Information/advice
3.3.1 Financial advice
3.3.2 Management information
3.3.3 Financial training
3.3.4 Performance review

Appendix B
The financing of local government

Introduction

Local authorities derive their revenue from:

- fees and charges for services provided (including housing rents);
- Government grants;
- business rates (which are set nationally but collected locally);
- local taxation – currently the Council tax.

In broad terms around 25 per cent of local authority revenue spending is covered by fees, charges and non-grant service income. The normal convention when looking at local authority spending is to concentrate on net revenue expenditure, which is gross revenue spending less income from fees and charges.

On this basis aggregate local authority net revenue expenditure in England during 1996/97 will be about £45 000 million. Nearly £23 000 million of this (51 per cent) will be covered by grants from central Government. A further £12 750 million (29 per cent) will be raised from the national non-domestic rate, leaving just over £9000 million (20 per cent) to be raised from the Council tax.

The Local Government Finance Act 1988 introduced a radically different system of funding for local government services which came into force in England and Wales in April 1990. The main changes were:

- to introduce a uniform national non-domestic rate for business;
- to employ a simplified system of paying central Government grants to local authorities;

- to abolish domestic rates and introduce a community charge on persons aged 18 and over. This was commonly known as the poll tax.

In the remainder of this Appendix we shall describe briefly the way in which the system has developed from that point. Readers should note that this entire Appendix deals exclusively with revenue expenditure; capital spending is dealt with in Appendix C.

The position before 1990

Until 1990 local authority revenue expenditure was funded by Government grants and rates. Rates were levied on domestic and non-domestic properties, with the rate levy for both being determined locally.

The 1980s saw a prolonged and active campaign on the part of central Government to control local authority spending and, in particular, to curb the perceived excesses of some individual local authorities. The introduction of rate capping in 1984 was followed rapidly by the abolition of the Greater London Council and the six metropolitan county councils. However, continuing Government disenchantment with local government finance culminated in the publication in 1986 of a Green Paper entitled 'Paying for Local Government'. The Green Paper catalogued the shortcomings of the system, with particular emphasis being placed on problems with local accountability, namely:

- the absence of a business vote despite the fact that non-domestic rates accounted for roughly half of local authority rate income;

- the fact that, of the 35 million local electors in England, only the 18 million householders paid rates and, because of rate rebates, only 12 million paid rates in full;

- the complexity and instability of the grants system and the consequential distortion of the link between local spending and local rates levels.

To remedy these shortcomings the Green Paper put forward the three major reforms listed earlier in this Appendix. In the face of considerable but fragmented hostility from the local authority side, the original package remainder intact and was eventually enacted in the 1988 Act. We shall now look at each element in turn.

Non-domestic rates

From April 1990 a uniform national non-domestic (business) rate has been levied throughout England. The basic amount due for a business property or hereditament is the product of its rateable value (RV) and a multiplier which is expressed as so many pence, e.g. 44.9 pence for 1996/97. This basic amount may be subject to various adjustments such as charitable relief or transitional relief. The multiplier is fixed by central Government at the start of each financial year and the year-on-year increase is limited to not more than the increase in the retail price index (RPI) for the year up to the preceding September. Billing authorities, i.e. unitary, district and borough councils, are responsible for the billing and collection of the national business rate.

The valuation of business property is not the responsibility of local authorities, but is carried out by the District Valuation Office, which is a branch of the Inland Revenue. A revaluation of all business property took place in 1989 and was effective from April 1990. Because there had been such a long gap since the previous revaluation in 1973, there was a massive (eight-fold on average) increase in RVs. Although this was offset by a corresponding reduction in the multiplier, so that the overall burden of business rates did not increase, the revaluation did create winners and losers in that certain types of property, e.g. small business premises, had much bigger RV increases than others, e.g. large industrial sites. A complex system of transitional relief has been in place ever since, despite the fact that there are now to be revaluations every five years so that new 1995 RVs are in the process of being introduced!

One issue which is now of crucial importance is whether a particular property is liable for the business rate. Not surprisingly, an intricate web of regulations and case law has already built up. A good example is the holiday home, where it has been deemed by regulation that a property should be classified as non-domestic if it is available for letting commercially for short periods totalling 140 days or more during the year.

The proceeds of the national non-domestic rate levy are treated as a national pool which is redistributed on the basis of a fixed amount per person. This mechanism redistributes the proceeds of the national business rate from areas of high rateable value but low resident population to those with low rateable value and high resident population, i.e. from urban and industrial areas to suburban and rural areas. In those shire areas where there are still two tiers of local government, the income from business rates is divided between the county and district councils in accordance with share of the national total of standard spending assessments (*see* below) which relates to the services which they provide.

Government grants

Of the £23 000 million total of Government grant to local authorities in 1996/97, some £18 000 or nearly 80 per cent is a general grant in support of all local authority services. It is now known as the revenue support grant, although it has had other titles in the recent past, such as block grant and standard spending grant. Since 1990 the grant entitlement for each local authority area has been calculated to enable all areas to levy the same local tax if they all spend at the level of their needs, as measured by their standard spending assessments (SSAs). Grant entitlements for each financial year are fixed in advance and do not vary with expenditure, which is a major change from the previous arrangements.

The needs assessment remains a key component of the grant system but since 1990 the Government has attempted to make it simpler and more stable. At that time the number of separate components of the needs assessment calculation was reduced by two-thirds to just over 20. This seemingly laudable objective may have overlooked the fact that the complexities of the previous needs assessment, which was known as the grant-related expenditure assessment or GREA, were the result of persistent efforts to achieve a fairer outcome. In this respect the quest for greater accountability was seriously flawed.

The £5000 million of Government grant to local authorities which is not distributed as revenue support grant is made up of specific grants and subsidies, with the Police Grant being the largest single component. The principles underlying specific grant support have already been discussed in Chapter 9.

Standard spending assessment

The present SSA system was introduced in 1990 and has been subject to some modifications since then, most recently in 1993. In 1996/97 SSAs total £40 000 million, although it must be emphasised that the figures used are notional. The SSA framework includes seven main service components – education, social services, police, fire, highways maintenance, other services and capital financing – with the first two of these being further sub-divided.

For most services the principle underlying the calculation of an SSA is fairly simple. A client group, is identified, e.g. number of primary school pupils, and is multiplied by an appropriate unit cost to give a notional spending figure. Adjustments may be made to the unit cost to reflect specific characteristics of the client group e.g. additional educational needs. There is also an area cost adjustment which is applied to most SSA components to take account of increased costs in London and the South East; this is an increasingly controversial aspect of SSA methodology!

In the case of the police, highways maintenance and capital financing, the client group approach is not applied. In the first case the number of police officers approved by the Home Office is the main indicator, and road lengths are used in the highways maintenance SSA. The capital financing assessment is based on the assumed level of outstanding debt, although the details are fairly complicated.

Where two-tier local government still exists, the SSA for 'other services' has to be split between county and district councils. It is not possible to give a concise and accurate description of how this is done. It should also be noted that there is no separate SSA for housing; this is because there is a totally separate national funding and accounting mechanism for most housing services.

As indicated previously, a review of SSAs was carried out in 1993, with the results being incorporated into the 1994/95 revenue support grant settlement. One of the main purposes of this exercise was to incorporate data from the 1991 census into the various SSA formulae. Some authorities, particularly in urban areas, faced significant SSA reductions as a result of this process. To protect these authorities from a catastrophic one-off reduction in Government grant, transitional protection was put in place in the form of an SSA reduction grant. Since 1994/95, this protection has been tapered down, but it still applies to some authorities in 1996/97.

The community charge

From April 1990 to March 1993, the community charge was the local tax which bridged the gap between the spending by all local authorities in a particular area and the amounts received in respect of business rates and standard spending grant, as it was then known. It took the form of a flat rate tax on all adults and was therefore popularly known as the poll tax. The official title of community charge was chosen presumably to avoid comparisons with much earlier but equally ill-fated poll tax experiments. However, the title also reflected the Government's wish that the payment should be regarded as a charge for local services, rather than a conventional tax.

Despite the very simple principle on which the community charge was based, there were a host of practical complications. First, as well as the personal community charge, there was a standard community charge for vacant property and second homes, and a collective community charge for rented and other accommodation in multiple residence where the turnover of residents was high. Secondly, not every adult was required to pay the full charge. The list of total or partial exemptions included:

- those aged under 19 still at school;

- resident National Health Service hospital patients;

- persons detained in mental hospitals;

- seriously mentally handicapped people;

- residents of nursing homes and hostels receiving care;

- prisoners (except those in prison for non-payments);

- the homeless and persons in night shelters or hostels;

- monks and nuns;

- residents of barracks and certain other Crown buildings;

- diplomats and members of visiting armed forces and their dependants;

- full-time students – liable for 20 per cent only;

- people on income support – liable for 20 per cent only.

Other features of the new system were the community charge register, which was separate from the electoral register, and the requirement for every adult to receive a separate bill in a separate envelope, even where two or more adults were resident at the same address.

The failure of the community charge is a matter of history. Once the impact of the new tax became known in spring 1990, there was considerable public resistance, which culminated in the poll tax riots in London during March of that year. There is no doubt that its unpopularity was one of the factors which sowed the seeds for Mrs Thatcher's resignation in the autumn of 1990 and, by December, a thorough review had been commissioned. In the March 1991 budget VAT was raised from 15 per cent to 17.5 per cent to fund a £4500 million reduction in community charge bills, which was equivalent to £140 per charge payer. In the same month the Secretary of State for the Environment announced the introduction from April 1993 of a new property-based tax, to be known as the Council tax.

There are many reasons for the spectacular failure of the community charge; indeed in hindsight it was a very bad and expensive mistake! Its introduction involved moving from a tax which, after allowing for rebates, was paid by 12 million householders to one where every one of the 40 million adults in the country was required to pay something. Considerable public resistance was therefore to be expected. The transition to the new system was also poorly managed in that there was no proper allowance nationally for implementation costs or for increased collection costs, including the impact of non-collection. This was compounded by a wholly inadequate provision for inflation within the local government finance settlement for 1990/91. As a result, councils were forced to set much higher levels of community charge than had been anticipated, which meant that most households had to pay more under the first year of the new system than they had under the last year of the old system. Almost immediately, therefore, public opinion labelled the community charge unfair, as well as bureaucratic and intrusive.

The Council tax

Although the Council tax is a property tax and has some similarities with the system of domestic rates which existed prior to 1990, there are a number of important differences.

Properties are now valued on the basis of capital, rather than rental, values. In other words the property valuation depends on how much it could be sold for, rather than the annual rent that could be earned by letting it. Also, properties are valued according to eight valuation bands as set out in Table B.1.

Table B.1

Band		Council tax factor
A	Up to £40 000	6
B	Over £40 000 and up to £52 000	7
C	Over £52 000 and up to £68 000	8
D	Over £68 000 and up to £88 000	9
E	Over £88 000 and up to £120 000	11
F	Over £120 000 and up to £160 000	13
G	Over £160 000 and up to £320 000	15
H	Over £320 000	18

The banding arrangement set out in Table B.1 is designed to make valuation more straightforward and to avoid the need for regular revaluations. The factors in the right hand column of the table are laid down in statute and determine the relative Council tax level for each valuation band. In practice they mean that, for example, the amount of Council tax for a Band H property in any area must always be twice the amount for a Band D property, and three times the amount for a Band A property, in the same area.

For discount purposes, it is convenient to regard the Council tax as having two components, a property component and a personal component, with each representing half of the bill. The personal component assumes that there are at least two adults resident at the property. If there is one adult, the total bill is discounted by 25 per cent and if there are no adults, the total bill is reduced by 50 per cent. In assessing whether a discount is appropriate, certain adults are disregarded, including 19-year-olds still at school and some students. Like business rates, Council tax is collected by unitary, district and borough councils. Part of the Council tax proceeds may have to be paid to precepting authorities such as county councils, police authorities, fire and civil defence authorities, and parish or town councils. Each billing authority is required to maintain a collection fund to deal with most of these transactions, and also to deal with the aftermath of the community charge.

Gearing

One of the key aspects of the post-1990 scenario is that central funding (grant plus the national business rate) now represents 80 per cent of local authority spending. The local tax base now represents only 20 per cent of spending compared with well over 50 per cent prior to 1990. Because the proceeds from business rates and Government grants are fixed any increase in local spending has to be met entirely from the local tax. This means that a 1 per cent increase in local authority spending requires a 5 per cent increase in local tax. This phenomenon is known as gearing and has been an important, although by no means welcome, feature of the new system.

Capping

Although capping was first introduced under the pre-1990 system of local government finance, which was based on rates, it has been continued and extended under the community charge and Council tax regimes. The basic principle of capping is that the Government, in the person of the Secretary of State for the Environment, can specify a maximum expenditure and tax or precept level for a Council, above which that Authority cannot go. Capping distorts the twin concepts of local autonomy and accountability, because it limits the extent to which an authority can make its own decisions about local spending and tax levels, and be held to account for them.

The legislation provides for capping to be applied to authorities whose expenditure is excessive, either in absolute terms, or in terms of the increase from one year to the next. The Secretary of State has wide discretion in setting the criteria for excessive spending. Originally, capping was applied retrospectively and affected only a limited number of authorities; those which breached the criteria for excessive spending in one financial year were capped in the next year. In the early stages, capping could not be applied to authorities spending less than £15 million per year, which exempted most shire district councils. Since 1990, however, capping has been applied at the start of each financial year to the budgets for that year and, with the removal of the *de minimis* limit, has affected the vast majority of authorities. Excessive spending is now defined by comparing an authority's budget with its SSA. The capping limit, i.e. the maximum budgeted expenditure level above which an authority cannot legally go, is also fixed by reference to the SSA and the last year's budget (often with some adjustment to reflect changes in role). In 1996/97, for the first time, the capping rules use individual service SSAs.

There has always been provision within the capping framework for any authority to apply to the Secretary of State for an increase in its capping limit, which is usually referred to as a redetermination. In each year since 1990, a small but significant number of authorities have made use of this facility, but not all have been successful. If an authority seeks a higher capping limit and bases its Council tax levy or precept on the higher limit, then a refusal by the Secretary of State to agree to this redetermination may well mean that budgets have to be revised and Council tax bills reissued, with the consequential delay, confusion and extra costs.

The combination of capping and gearing represents a much more effective mechanism than ever before for influencing local authority spending decisions. In particular, the effect of capping has been to move local authority budgets towards their SSAs. However, most authorities continue to spend above their SSA, and in some cases substantial cuts in services would still be required to 'achieve' the SSA!

Appendix C

The definition and control of capital expenditure

Introduction

Capital expenditure has for some time been one of the most problematic and least satisfactory areas of local government finance. There has been longstanding controversy and confusion about:

- **definition** – how to define capital spending and, in particular, how to achieve a clear distinction between capital and revenue spending;

- **capital controls** – the justification for, and the nature and extent of government controls over capital spending by local authorities;

- **capital accounting** – how best to present capital assets and capital transactions in local authority accounts, and how best to reflect capital asset usage in service costs.

Definition of capital expenditure

Before venturing further it is advisable to review the basic ideas which underpin the separate treatment of capital spending. To the layman there is no intrinsic difference between capital and revenue spending. In either case money is paid out to acquire a commodity or service which will be of use to the organisation. However there is a distinction between capital and revenue spending and it lies in the following characteristics:

- the scale of the transaction;

- the nature of the commodity or service acquired;

- how the money is obtained to pay for the commodity or service, i.e. the method of finance.

Table C.1 highlights the difference. The first criterion is based on practice rather than theory. The scale of a transaction should not determine whether expenditure is capital or revenue. In practice, however, capital expenditure necessitates more record-keeping. Small transactions are often assumed therefore to be *de minimis* and are treated as revenue expenditure. It is a grave admission for professional accountants to confess to such a pragmatic approach!

Table C.1

	Capital spending	Revenue spending
Scale of work	Relatively large	Relatively small
Nature of work	Of long-term value	Consumed immediately or of only short-term value
Method of finance	External loan	Revenue resources
Example	Building a new school	Wages of cleaning staff

As far as the second of these criteria is concerned, the distinction is one of degree. There is no clear boundary which can be applied and this leads to some overlapping in practice. For example, the acquisition of a small piece of land perhaps costing no more than £5000 would be deemed capital expenditure whereas a £50 000 bill for the consumption of electricity would be a revenue cost. The purchase of a book would always be classified as revenue expenditure even though it could have a longer useful life than a mechanical road sweeper which would usually be treated as capital expenditure. If, however, an authority is stocking a new library with a large supply of books, that expenditure might well be classified as capital outlay.

The third criterion, method of finance, is a logical extension of the first two, particularly to non-accountants. If an individual or organisation is contemplating the acquisition of a very costly item, it may simply be a matter of necessity for the transaction to be funded by a loan. Even if there is sufficient money in the bank to meet the entire cost of the acquisition it may well be sensible to take out a loan and thereby spread the cost over a period of years. As well as assisting cash flow in the short term, this will allow the payments profile to be matched against the flow of benefits which the asset will provide. This scenario emphasises the investment nature of most capital spending by corporate organisations, including local authorities.

External borrowing by local authorities is subject to a variety of statutory constraints. One of the most important is that local authorities are not allowed to borrow for revenue purposes (except on a very short-term basis). Any expenditure funded by borrowing will thus be capital expenditure. The reverse is not true however, as many local authorities fund significant amounts of capital spending each year from their revenue budgets. Non-finance managers should be aware therefore that the link between capital expenditure and borrowing is not absolute.

So far we have tried to explain the nature of local authority capital expenditure. However, there remains the need for a rigorous definition and this can now be found in the Local Government and Housing Act 1989, which introduced the present capital control regime and applies the 'capital' label to the following categories of expenditure:

- the acquisition of land and the acquisition or replacement of buildings, vehicles, plant, machinery and equipment;

- the construction of buildings and roads, the installation of plant, machinery and equipment and the enhancement of property;

- grants or loans to support capital spending by other persons;

- investments (excluding trust funds and temporary deposits) and the acquisition of share capital.

A key element of this approach is the attempt to distinguish clearly between the enhancement or improvement of property, and repairs and maintenance to property, which has been a persistent 'grey area' in the past. Enhancement is now deemed to include any expenditure which substantially:

- lengthens the life of an asset; or

- increases its market value; or

- extends its existing use.

Such expenditure is within the definition of capital expenditure. However this statutory definition does not include repairs and maintenance. Expenditure on repairs and maintenance is therefore a revenue cost. This means in principle that:

- it cannot be classified as capital expenditure;

- it is not subject to capital controls;

- it cannot be financed by borrowing.

Capital controls

The capital control system in place before 1990 sought to control the amount a local authority spent in any financial year for capital purposes. It was singularly unsuccessful in achieving most of the Government's stated objectives, which were:

- to provide the Government with an effective means of influencing local authority capital expenditure and borrowing;

- to ensure that the distribution of capital spending reflects both national and local needs;

- to encourage asset sales and thereby reduce the size of the public sector;

- to enable local authorities to plan capital programmes with reasonable certainty;

- to reduce the overall level of local authority debt.

Local authority CFOs are an inventive breed and they contrived various legal devices which increased local flexibility at the expense of some of the above objectives. These include advanced purchase schemes, deferred purchase schemes, sale or lease and leaseback arrangements, barter, in-and-out schemes and the cascade principle.

Consequently a different capital control system was introduced in the Local Government and Housing Act 1989 and took effect from April 1990. The system was intended to be simpler than its predecessor had become and to shore up the 'deficiencies' in the 1980 system. It is based mainly on controlling what may be borrowed in each financial year, which, incidentally, is how local authority capital spending was controlled before 1980.

The key component of the new system is the credit approval. Each local authority receives a basic credit approval (BCA) before the start of the financial year which limits the authority's level of borrowing in that year to finance capital expenditure. Supplementary credit approvals may be issued during or even after the end of the financial year to which they relate. Credit approvals also apply to credit arrangements other than borrowing, e.g. leases.

As before, capital receipts provide a mechanism for enhancing capital expenditure beyond the limits imposed by credit approvals. In simple terms a capital receipt is the cash or other consideration received when an asset, e.g. land or buildings, is disposed of. Under the present legislation, a proportion of capital receipts must be set aside as provision to repay debt. This reflects both the fact that there may be outstanding debt on an asset when it is disposed of, and the Government's determination to control overall local authority indebtedness as part of its campaign to reduce the public sector borrowing requirement. The usable proportion of a capital receipt, i.e. the amount which can be used to justify new capital expenditure, was initially set at 25 per cent for receipts from council house sales and 50 per cent from other receipts. However, there are a variety of circumstances in which the usable proportion can be increased, some of which cover asset replacement and in-and-out schemes. In addition the rules have been subject to various temporary relaxations in the light of pressures for increased capital spending.

An authority's BCA for the year is issued by the Department for the Environment and covers all services. However, it is calculated on the basis of capital guideline figures for each main service area which are issued by the relevant Government departments in response to annual bids by individual authorities. For example each LEA makes an annual capital submission to the DFEE in the autumn, which is used to allocate the total national planning figure for education capital spending in the next financial year. These annual LEA submissions reflect the need for capital spending on schools in each area, but also take into account known national priorities, e.g. to rationalise surplus school places.

Annual capital guidelines (ACGs) are issued for five main service blocks – education, housing, transport, social services and other services. An authority's BCA is the sum of its ACGs, subject to a deduction for its assumed ability to finance capital spending from usable capital receipts. Inevitably ACGs are invariably much lower than an authority has bid for, whereas the figure for 'receipts taken into account', as the deduction is now known, is always higher than CFOs believe it should be! The end result is that local authority capital spending in recent years has totally failed to keep pace with the need to preserve and improve the buildings and other assets which are used to deliver local services.

Financing capital expenditure

If an individual wants to buy a house, he or she must borrow money from a bank or building society, persuade a benevolent third party to foot the bill, use his or her own savings or, more usually, apply the proceeds from selling an existing property to fund the purchase. Any combination of these options is also possible. In exactly the same way, capital spending by a local authority can be financed in five ways:

- borrowing or other credit arrangements, such as leasing of property and equipment;

- capital receipts;

- Government grants or contributions/donations from third parties;

- the authority's own funds, e.g. replacement or capital funds;

- direct revenue funding.

Under the present capital control system, any capital expenditure which is financed by borrowing or other credit arrangements counts against an authority's credit approval. The position with regard to capital receipts has already been covered.

Capital spending which is financed by grants or contributions is free from control. It must be emphasised that this applies only to contributions or donations from third parties; it does not apply to loans from third parties which do count against the credit limit.

Where the authority uses a replacement or capital fund, the relevant capital expenditure also does not count against the credit approval. This applies also to direct revenue funding, which traditionally has been described as 'revenue contributions to capital outlay' (RCCO). However, it is important to understand precisely what is meant by 'direct revenue funding'; for such expenditure to be free from control it must be charged in full to the revenue account in the year during which it is incurred. At the corporate level the use of direct revenue financing is obviously limited by the impact it has on the Council tax (gearing) and the existence of capping (*see* Appendix B).

Capital accounting

The traditional approach to capital accounting was to include charges within service budgets which were based on the costs of servicing any debt on the assets employed, i.e principal and interest repayments, or the leasing/rental costs of those assets. To the extent that the assets concerned had been financed by direct revenue funding, no charge was made for the use of that asset.

This approach patently failed to reflect in local authority accounts the true cost of employing capital assets. It undermined the comparability between local authority financial statements and those generated by the private sector.

In addition, it severely limited the value of local authority financial statements in informing decisions about resource allocation.

In the face of Government pressure, CIPFA developed a new system of capital accounting which came into effect on 1 April 1994 and has now been incorporated within its Code of Practice on Local Authority Accounting

The basic principle of the new system is that budgets and financial statements for services which employ fixed assets now include capital charges based on asset valuations. These charges include an element to cover the cost of wearing out or consumption of the asset (depreciation) and an element to cover the opportunity cost of the capital resources tied up in the asset (interest).

The new arrangements require every local authority to value all of its capital assets and to establish and maintain an assets register. It may be surprising and somewhat alarming to learn that this has proved an onerous task for most authorities, and has been one of the main reasons why CIPFA has had to fight long and hard to establish the new system.

Another transitional problem is the fact that the new basis of calculating capital charges leads to much higher levels of charge than the old basis. The reported costs of most local authority services have therefore increased significantly. To prevent a catastrophic and unintended increase in overall local authority expenditure, some 'below the line' accounting adjustments are required. Local authority accounts now include a credit for the total of capital charges to service accounts, and a debit for the traditional capital financing charges which still have to be paid. These adjustments reflect the fact that the new capital charges do not, in the main, involve money changing hands.

Footnote

There is a fundamental weakness of all capital control systems, past and present, namely the annual nature of capital controls. Whatever the justification for Government control over local authority capital spending, it is surely fair to argue that the planning of capital investment requires some reasonable idea of future prospects in the medium and long term. For this exercise to be at the mercy of an annual rationing process which, based on past experience, is neither stable nor predictable must surely remain one of the more bizarre characteristics of local government finance.

Appendix D

Service level agreements and a framework for support services

OBJECTIVES

The aims of this Appendix are

■ to summarise very briefly some of the issues which need to be covered in drawing up and implementing SLAs for financial management functions;

■ to put forward a broad corporate framework to encompass all support services, whether or not they are covered by SLAs (as discussed in Chapter 9).

Service level agreements

The principal matters that must be covered in an SLA are:

(a) the period of the agreement;

(b) the scope of the agreement – the broad functions which it covers, e.g. payroll, creditor payments, income, financial advice, internal audit;

(c) the detailed terms and conditions under which each function will be performed (*see* below);

(d) the basis on which charges will be calculated and levied (*see* below);

(e) arrangements for extension or renewal of the agreement, including a mechanism for identifying the client's future needs;

(f) notice periods for varying or terminating the agreement;

(g) monitoring arrangements;

(h) arbitration procedures in the event of a dispute;

(i) procedures and penalties in the event of poor performance or default.

The terms and conditions referred to at (c) above will have three principal components:

■ a detailed specification of the services to be provided;

■ a list of requirements that must be met, and by whom, so that the CFO can fulfil his or her statutory responsibility (*see* Chapter 2); these are described as 'minimum requirements'. They need not be part of the SLA itself and might instead be appended to financial regulations or form a separate supporting manual of financial instructions;

■ details of any performance standards that will apply.

The service specification is a vital part of any SLA. Reasonable efforts should be made to ensure this is as clear and comprehensive as possible, although it must be borne in mind that very lengthy and tortuous statements are unlikely to be helpful. In our experience, clients find it particularly helpful if the specification spells out, where appropriate, the guaranteed minimum level of service. It is also important to make clear in the specification which elements of the service are provided automatically on a continuous or predetermined basis, which are available on demand and which are only available if particular circumstances arise or at the discretion of the service provider.

There are various bases on which charges can be calculated. These include:

■ **A fixed fee**   A single fee could cover all the services provided or separate fees could be agreed for each activity.

■ **A banded charge**   This is an extension of the fixed fee whereby the fee increases in discrete steps according to the workload on a particular function. There would need to be a separate scale of charges for each function.

■ **Unit charges**   Unit charges such as £x per payroll employee or y pence per creditor invoice could be charged. Such unit charges might be based either on:

  – **average cost** – the total cost of carrying out the function, including fixed costs, divided by the number of units;

  – **marginal cost** – the variable cost per unit or the additional cost which would be incurred if the workload increased by one unit.

If a marginal cost basis were used to set the unit charges there would also need to be a lump sum fee, to cover fixed costs.

It may be appropriate for the statement of charges to include a mechanism for dealing with inflation. Numerous alternatives are available; our preference would be to increase charges in line with the April pay award for administrative, professional and clerical staff. The alternative would be a cash-limit approach whereby charges were fixed for a given period (say one year). Provision would then have to be made for periodic reviews.

Considerable care needs to be taken in setting up the framework of charges. In particular account should be taken of:

- **Risk**   The greater the fixed element of any charge, the fewer the problems caused to the service provider by a reduction in service activity. However, the converse also applies and a high fixed fee element is vulnerable to higher than expected increases in work volumes.

- **Incentives**   Unit charges which reflect the differences in resource input to each process can be a means of encouraging the client department to limit their demand for processes which impose high costs on the provider, e.g. submitting invoices for urgent payment.

- **Data requirements**   The more sophisticated the charging basis used, the greater the volume of data which are likely to be required to calculate the charges. This could impose a significant burden on the provider's staff in collecting and recording the data, and on staff in the client department who have to monitor and verify the charges.

Numerous practical examples of SLAs now abound in every local authority. It is suggested that the best examples will have the following characteristics:

- a focus on outputs or outcomes;

- a reference to all relevant outcomes, not just those that are easy to measure;

- a minimum of jargon;

- a clear explanation of the choices available and how these are exercised;

- well-defined and effective customer liaison and feedback arrangements;

- an explicit and genuine commitment to be as responsive and flexible as possible.

A framework for support services

Although SLAs are now very common in local government, they are not, in our view, well understood by many of the elected members and officers who are affected by them. This is not because they are inherently complicated but, in the first place, because they have probably been developed in a reactive and piecemeal fashion. As a result of this piecemeal approach, the range of support services covered by SLAs varies considerably from one local authority to another. In addition, it is quite likely that, within a single authority, the development of SLAs will have been patchy; it may even be the case that certain support services are subject to SLAs, despite the fact that this is inappropriate.

Although we do not consider that all support services should be covered by SLAs, we do believe that, in order to avoid the confusion and misunderstanding which exists in some authorities, there should be a common framework across an authority for managing the delivery of all support services. This should, in our view, be based on:

■ Partnership – each department and team working together to achieve quality services to the public;

■ Openness – maximum sharing of information, ideas and problems;

■ Accountability – effective monitoring and feedback on performance and costs.

This framework should cover all those services which departments provide to support the operation of other departments or establishments of the authority (including LMS schools in the case of LEAs), except for services covered by the CIPFA definition of service strategy and regulation, and any services which are controlled corporately and budgeted for separately. This framework can also be operated within departments, i.e. to the services provided by one team or unit on behalf of other teams or units in the same department. We must make it absolutely clear, however, that we are not advocating internal SLAs within departments; indeed it seems to us that developing SLAs to this extent may be counter-productive as the cost and burden of the extra paperwork could well outweigh any potential efficiency gains.

Within the corporate framework, all support services should be covered by SLAs, as previously described, or by service level statements (SLSs). An SLS is similar to an SLA in that it must include a detailed service specification and a clear statement of the basis on which the service will be charged for. However, an SLS will apply to those situations where the client has no freedom to choose an alternative provider, and has little or no choice, at least in the short term, over the nature and level of service provided. Consequently, there is no need to include in an SLS details about start dates, renewal and termination procedures, penalty clauses or arbitration arrangements. Performance monitoring and customer liaison procedures should, if possible, be covered, so that the client or service user can give informed feedback on performance and be able to influence the future development of the service.

A key requirement of the corporate framework is that all support services should operate within a financial structure which makes clear where the budgetary responsibilities lie. In addition, the type of agreement employed in each case, i.e. SLA or SLS, must be compatible with the actual budgetary arrangements. A possible structure is as set out in Table D.1.

Table D.1

Category	Description	Budget responsibility	Type of agreement
Delegation	Client has choice about provider and level of service	Client	SLA
Devolution	Identified budget must be used for specified purpose but client can choose supplier	Client	SLA/SLS
Allocation	Costs are allocated on the basis of actual usage	Provider	SLS
Apportionment	Costs are shared out on fixed or formula basis	Provider	SLS

It must be stressed that what has been outlined in Table D.1 is merely a mechanism for managing support services, not a radical new approach to this issue. The potential benefits of a clear corporate structure, such as the one we have described, are that it:

- provides a clear and well-understood relationship between all support service providers and users;

- promotes a culture of openness and mutual trust in the management and delivery of support services;

- encourages informed discussion about the future development of support services.

Glossary of financial terms

Most of this glossary is reproduced from the Local Authority Finance Glossary published by the Chartered Institute of Public Finance and Accountancy.

Accounts: a generic term for statements setting out details of income and expenditure over an accounting period (usually a year) or assets and liabilities at the end of the period, or both, in a structured manner

Accruals: an important accountancy concept which recognises that income and expenditure may well be incurred before money is received or paid out

Aggregate exchequer grant (AEG): the total amount of government grant made available each year to local government. It comprises a general grant, now known as revenue support grant, and certain specific grants

Aggregate external finance (AEF): the total of central support for local authorities' revenue expenditure. It comprises government grants and income from the uniform national non-domestic rate

Annual capital guidelines (ACGs): the separate assessment by the relevant Government department of the relative need for each local authority to incur capital expenditure in a financial year in five service areas – education, housing, social services, transport and other services

Appropriation: the transfer of ownership of land or a building that is no longer required by one local authority service to another

Asset: something of worth which is measurable in monetary terms, e.g. land, buildings, equipment, goodwill

Asset rent: an annual charge to the user of a fixed asset, based on a suitable valuation of that asset

Audit: an independent examination of an organisation's activities, either by internal audit or the organisation's external auditor

Audit Commission: an independent body created by the Local Government Finance Act 1982 with responsibility for the external audit of all local authority accounts from 1 April 1983

Auditor's opinion: the opinion that is required by statute from an authority's external auditors, indicating whether the audit has been completed in accordance with Part III of the Local Government Act 1982 and the Code of Audit Practice, and also whether the statement of accounts presents fairly the financial position of the authority

Balance sheet: a statement of the recorded assets and liabilities at a specific date at the end of an accounting period

Balances: the capital or revenue reserves of an authority made up of the accumulated surplus of income over expenditure on the general fund, county fund, collection fund or any other fund

Billing authority: a unitary, borough or district council with the statutory responsibility for the collection of the Council tax and the national non-domestic rate. Such authorities are also referred to as charging authorities

Budget: a statement of an authority's forecast of net revenue and capital expenditure over a specified period of time

Budget head: each section of the budget for which estimates are produced and over which budgetary control is exercised

Business plan: a plan covering a specified future period (usually more than one year) which sets out an organisation's objectives, forecasts and resource requirements, and may also include targets or performance standards against which achievements can be measured

Capital accounts: the accounts which record all transactions relating to capital expenditure and income. Local authorities keep these accounts on the basis of receipts and payments made in the accounting period

Capital controls: the various methods by which the level of capital expenditure is controlled by central government

Capital employed: the assets used by an organisation to undertake its activities

Capital expenditure: expenditure on the acquisition or enhancement of fixed assets or which otherwise will be of use or benefit to an authority in providing its services beyond the year of account (*see also* Appendix C)

Capital financing: the raising of money to pay for capital expenditure. It covers borrowing, leasing, revenue contributions to capital outlay, capital receipts, capital grants, capital fund and other contributions

Capital fund: an internal reserve to finance capital expenditure without resort to external borrowing

Capital programme: the capital projects an authority proposes to undertake over a stated period of time

Capital receipt: proceeds from the sale of a fixed asset, e.g. land or a building. Capital receipts can be used to repay debt or to finance new capital expenditure

Capping: the term originally applied to the provisions of the Rates Act 1984, by which the Government set rate or precept limits for specified authorities whose expenditure was deemed to be 'excessive'. From April 1990 it was succeeded by community charge capping under the terms of the Local Government Finance Act 1988. It has since been updated to reflect the introduction of Council tax

Cash limit: a method of expenditure control which restricts the amount which can be used for spending for a particular purpose to a specified amount, regardless of the effects of inflation

Central establishment charges: *see* Support services

Collection fund: a statutory fund which must be operated by every billing authority to account for most of its receipts and payments in respect of the Council tax and the national non-domestic rate

Commitment accounting: a system whereby transactions are recorded at the time the commitment arises. Commitments are initially recorded when orders are issued or received and are deleted when invoices are paid or money received, at which time the transaction will be recorded in the traditional way

Committed expenditure: expenditure in respect of goods,

services and works for which orders have been placed or tenders accepted but for which payment has not yet been made

Community charge: the local tax which replaced domestic rates in April 1990. It took the form of a flat-rate tax on all adults and was also known as the poll tax. In 1993 it was replaced by the Council tax

Contingency: a provision within the accounts for a future event whose financial impact is likely to be significant but is uncertain

Continuation budget: the cost of continuing existing policies and standards of service provision in a future year, before developments or reductions, expressed at a specified price base

Core function: a financial management function which is retained under the direct control of the CFO either to enable his or her statutory role as responsible financial officer to be fulfilled, or on the grounds of efficiency

Cost centre: the term for each individual unit to which items of income and expenditure are charged for either managerial or detailed control purposes, e.g. a vehicle or school

Council tax: a property-based tax introduced in 1993 to replace the community charge. It applies to domestic property. The level of Council tax is determined by the charge set by the billing authority and the valuation band in which a particular dwelling is placed. The amount payable is reduced if there are less than two adults living in a property

Credit approval: an authorisation to use borrowing or other credit arrangement to finance capital expenditure. This borrowing control has been in place since April 1990

Creditor: an amount owed for work done, goods received, or services rendered before the end of the accounting period, but for which payment has not been made by the end of that accounting period. The term is also used to describe the individual or organisation to whom the money is owed

Current asset: an asset where the value may change because the volume held can vary through day-to-day activity, e.g. physical stockholdings

Current expenditure: the direct revenue cost of local authority service provision; it excludes indirect costs such as capital financing costs

Current liability: an amount which will become payable or could be called in within the next accounting period, e.g. creditor, cash overdrawn (*see* Liability)

Debt charges: annual charges to the revenue accounts of a local authority to cover the interest on, and repayment of, loans for capital expenditure; a major component of capital financing costs

Debt outstanding: amounts borrowed, principally to finance capital expenditure or working capital, which are still to be repaid

Debtor: an amount due for work done, goods provided or services rendered, receivable by the end of the accounting period, but for which reimbursement has not, at that time, been received. The term is also used to describe the individual or organisation from whom the money is due

Depreciation: the theoretical loss in value of an asset due to age, wear and tear, deterioration, or obsolescence. Depreciation is charged to profit and loss, trading or revenue accounts to reflect asset usage

Direct service organisation (DSO): an organisation which consists of people directly employed by an authority (including supervisory and support staff, and their accommodation, equipment, etc.) to carry out work which is subject to CCT

Estimates: the forecasts of expenditure and income for a future accounting period (*see* Budget)

Financial regulations: a written code agreed by an authority to provide a framework within which to conduct its financial affairs. The regulations govern the procedures to be followed by all managers in relation to financial functions and they are intended to ensure financial integrity (probity)

Fixed asset: an asset which has value beyond one financial year

Fixed cost: a cost which does not vary directly with the volume of service or the number of units produced, e.g. plant and premises costs will not usually vary in the short term

General fund: the central fund of a billing authority into which all receipts are paid and from which all liabilities are met other than those relating to the collection fund. The cost of most of the services provided by the authority is met from this fund. In county councils the fund is traditionally referred to as the county fund

Grant related expenditure assessment (GREA): an assessment by government of how much each individual local authority would have to spend to provide a common level of service; it was replaced by the standard spending assessment in April 1990

Gross expenditure: the cost of providing services before the deduction of government grants or other income

Hereditament: a unit of property capable of separate occupation which would be shown as a separate item on the valuation lists for rating and Council tax purposes

Historic cost: amounts recorded at their original cost, and not adjusted for the effect of subsequent price changes or depreciation

Housing benefits: a national system of financial assistance to individuals towards certain housing costs, which is administered by local authorities on behalf of central Government.

Assistance takes the form of rent rebates and rent allowances

Housing revenue account (HRA): an account which includes the expenditure and income arising in connection with the provision of housing accommodation by a local authority

Housing subsidy: Government grant payable to housing authorities towards the cost of the provision of local authority housing and its management and maintenance

Inflation provision: an allowance within a budget which is designed to cover variations in costs of providing services from the price base at which the budget was prepared to the end of the accounting period

Insurance fund: an internal reserve created to provide finance to make good, in whole or in part, loss or damage suffered by the authority

Interest: an amount received or paid for the use of a sum of money when it is invested or borrowed

Joint board: a legally separate body with a power to levy a precept, comprising representatives of two or more local authorities. Joint boards exist in the metropolitan areas and London to provide certain services which were administered by metropolitan county councils or the Greater London Council prior to their abolition, e.g. the fire service

Leasing: a method of financing capital expenditure under which a rental charge is paid for an asset for a specified period of time. A finance lease transfers the risks and rewards of ownership of a fixed asset to the lessee. An operating lease does not

Liability: an amount due to an individual or organisation which will be paid at some time in the future. Liabilities include debt outstanding and creditors

Loans fund: a fund into which borrowed monies are paid and from which advances are made to individual capital accounts to finance capital expenditure instead of raising earmarked loans for each individual item

Loans outstanding: the total amounts borrowed from external lenders for capital and temporary revenue purposes but not repaid at the balance sheet date

Management accounting: the provision of information, particularly costing information, primarily to aid decision-making

Minimum standards: the minimum levels of control, e.g. authorisations, checks, required by the CFO, as responsible finance officer, to be applied to each non-core financial management function to ensure financial integrity (probity)

Multiplier: the national factor applied to rateable value to determine the rates due for each non-domestic property. Under the pre-1990 system, it used to be known as the rate levy or poundage. The multiplier is fixed by Government, subject to a statutory limit on its year-on-year increase

National non-domestic rate: the contribution towards the cost of local authority services by business ratepayers. The proceeds of the national rate payable on business properties is collected by billing authorities but paid into a national pool. It is then redistributed as a fixed amount per adult

Needs assessment: an amount of revenue expenditure, net of specific grants, which the Government considers appropriate for each authority to incur in providing a common standard of service. It is an annual judgement by Government reflecting not only the local circumstances of each area, but also factors affecting costs and government spending priorities. It is now known as the standard spending assessment (SSA)

Net assets: the total assets of an organisation less its liabilities

Net expenditure: the cost of providing a service after the deduction of specific grants and other sources of income but before deducting revenue support grant and Council tax income

Out-turn: the actual expenditure and income for a particular year of account, or other accounting period

Out-turn prices: the actual level of prices encountered during an accounting period

Overheads: expenses not directly incurred by a service or establishment but charged by way of an agreed procedure

Precept: a statutory demand by which a non-billing authority obtains the income it requires from the appropriate billing authorities to meet its net expenditure requirements, after taking account of its receipts from Government grants and the national non-domestic rate

Price base: the levels of pay and prices for goods and services at a specified date

Public expenditure: the combined spending of central and local government together with government loans and grants to public utilities

Public Works Loan Board (PWLB): a government agency which provides long-term loans to local authorities at interest rates only slightly higher than those at which the Government itself can borrow

Rate of return: under CCT legislation, the Government sets a target rate of return, usually expressed as a percentage of capital employed, for each DSO operated by an authority. Failure to achieve the target rate of return for three successive years may result in a government directive to wind up the DSO

Rateable value: the annual assumed rental value of a hereditament; it now applies only to non-domestic property. Rateable values are assessed by the District Valuation Officer, are subject to appeal and are reviewed every five years

Real terms spending: a level of spending over a period of time, measured on a constant price basis by eliminating the effects of inflation over the period concerned

Recharge: the transfer of costs from one account to another

Recoupment: the inter-authority charges which arise when one local authority educates pupils which are the responsibility of another. It now applies only to children with special educational needs

Rent allowance: a subsidy payable by a local authority to a low-income tenant or sub-tenant in private rented accommodation

Rent rebate: a subsidy payable by a local authority to low-income tenants in local authority accommodation

Repairs and renewal fund: a fund an authority can establish to meet the cost of repairing, maintaining, replacing and renewing its buildings, vehicles, plant and equipment

Reserve: amounts included in one period's accounts when the goods or services have been supplied/received but the actual receipt/payment occurs in a future accounting period

Revenue account: an account that records an authority's day-to-day expenditure and income on such items as salaries and wages, running costs of services and the financing costs of capital expenditure

Revenue contribution to capital outlay (RCCO): a charge to the revenue account to finance capital expenditure. The charge must be made in full within the same accounting period

Revenue expenditure: the day-to-day costs an authority incurs in providing services

Revenue support grant: a general grant paid to support all local authority services. It is the successor to the rate support grant and the standing spending grant. It is distributed on the basis of spending need as assessed by Government and it enables the same level of Council tax to be levied in each area for spending at standard spending assessment. Under the system of local government finance introduced in April 1993, revenue support grant is paid only in support of expenditure up to the level of the needs or SSA

Revised estimates: the approved estimates for the current year, as updated during that year

Running expenses: the day-to-day running costs an authority incurs in providing services, but specifically excluding direct employee expenses, capital financing costs and revenue contributions to capital outlay

Safety net: a device introduced into the revenue support grant system to limit grant losses or gains from one year to the next

Service level agreement (SLA): a written agreement setting out the terms and conditions under which one organisation or department provides services to another

Sinking fund: a fund created for the redemption of a liability or with the object of replacing an asset by setting aside a sum periodically and investing it so as to produce the required amount at the appropriate time

Specific grants: Government grants to local authorities in aid of particular projects or services

Standard spending assessment (SSA): *see* Needs assessment

Standing orders: formal rules an authority draws up to regulate its proceedings and the conduct of its business

Statement of accounts: the published accounts of an authority on which the external auditor gives an opinion. Under the Local Government Finance Act 1982, authorities are required to publish their statements of accounts within nine months of the end of each financial year

Subjective analysis: the classification of expenditure and income according to the nature of the transaction, e.g. salaries, fuel, telephones

Superannuation fund: a fund comprising sums deducted from employees' pay and employers' contributions, from which a range of pension benefits is paid to retired contributors, their widows and, where appropriate, dependent children

Supplementary estimate: an increase to a budget head during a year, approved in accordance with an authority's financial regulations

Supplementary grants: grants paid by Government to authorities on the basis of approved eligible expenditure on particular services, e.g. national parks

Support services: look up activities of a professional, technical and administrative nature, which are not local authority services in their own right, but give technical, organisational and administrative support to those services

Suspense account: an account which is used for receipts or payments that cannot immediately be allocated because of inadequate information

Temporary loan: money borrowed for an initial period of less than one year

Trust funds: assets owned by an individual or organisation and administered by an authority on their behalf

Valuation band: under the Council tax all domestic property is valued into bands that represent the sale value of the property. There are eight valuation bands and a separate Council tax amount applies to each band, with properties in higher value bands being subject to higher amounts. The relative differences in tax between each band are fixed by statute

Value for money: an expression describing the benefit obtained for a given input of resources (not just in financial terms)

Variable costs: a cost which varies directly with the volume of service or the number of units produced, e.g. food costs

Virement: the transfer of an uncommitted amount or underspending on one budget head to finance additional spending on another budget head, in accordance with an authority's financial regulations

Working capital: the sums available to meet day-to-day expenses. Working capital is usually calculated as current assets less current liabilities

Work in progress: the cost of work done on an uncompleted project at a specified date so far as it has not been recharged or recovered at that date

Index

accountability 8, 12, 112
accounts
    annual reports 80–1
    capital accounting 139–40
    final accounts 79
    overheads 12, 107
    preparation 14–15
Accounts and Audit Regulations 10, 88
advisory roles of chief financial officers 96–7
allocating costs 12, 107
annual capital guidelines (ACGs) 138
annual reports 80–1
annual revenue budgets 73–6
anti-competitive behaviour 42–3
apportioning costs 12, 107
asset management 91–2
Attorney General v De Winton 9
Audit Commission 4, 35, 79, 87–9, 99
audits
    external 87–9
    internal 10, 13–14, 85–7
    objectives 85–6, 88

BACS (electronic fund transfer) 64
basic credit approvals (BCA) 137, 138
benchmarking 100–1
bidding culture 104–6
borrowing
    and capital expenditure 139
    requirements 82, 83–4
    statutory constraints 136
budget holders 19, 21
budgetary control 77–9
budgets
    and accounts preparation 12, 14–15
    annual revenue budgets 73–6
    capital budgeting 76
    commitments system 52, 78
    and information technology (IT) 50
    profiling 78
business plans 24, 37–9, 90–1
business rates 67–8, 127

capital budgeting 76

capital expenditure 38, 134–40
    accounting 139–40
    control systems 137–8, 140
    definition 134–5
    financing 138–9
capping 132–3
cash flow 38, 60, 82–3
cash-limited budgeting 75–6
centralised structures 3
change xv, 6
charges under service level agreements 142–3
Chartered Institute of Public Finance and
        Accountancy (CIPFA) 4, 9, 11–12, 85, 101
chief financial officers
    core functions 11–17, 120
    relationship with ratepayers 9–10
    responsibilities 7–11
Chinese walls 33
Citizens Charter 34, 99–100, 106
Code of Audit Practice 88
codes of practice 9
commitment budgeting 75
commitments system of budgets 52, 78
communications *see* information technology
        (IT)
community charge 65, 68, 70, 104, 129–31
competition xv, 28, 113–15
    see also compulsory competitive tendering
        (CCT)
complaints 16
compulsory competitive tendering (CCT)
    anti-competitive behaviour 42–3
    assessment of 44
    awarding of contracts 28
    and capital spending 38
    and change of government 29
    and chief financial officers 31–2
    client agent role 30
    cost savings 28
    culture and relationships 32–5
    decentralising 3
    external audits 32
    financial management under 35–40
    and information needs 6

compulsory competitive tendering (CCT) –
    contd
  and insurance 38–9
  legislation 27
  local authority tasks 29–30
  purchaser/provider split 33, 106
  and the Secretary of State 32
  ꞮꝬꞥꞥꞲꞲꞲ ꞲꞲ ꞞꞲꞲꞲꞲꞲꞲꞲꞲꞲꞲ ꞲꞲꞲꞲꞲꞲꞲꞲꞲꞲ
      (TUPE) 43
  white-collar services 41–2
computer security 55–6
construction services 41, 42
continuation budgeting 74–5
control systems for capital expenditure 137–8,
    140
corporate strategy 24, 37–9, 90–1
corruption 8, 9
cost/benefit analysis 90
costs
  allocating 12, 107
  of benefit schemes 63
  of cash flow management 83
  of decentralising 6
  information on 108–9
  of information technology (IT) 46, 47
  of local authority business 10
  of non-domestic rate collection 68
  overheads 12, 107
  reducing xv, 24, 104
  savings under compulsory competitive
      tendering 28
  unit costs 98
Council tax 68–70, 104, 131–2
  means-tested benefits 62–3
  statutory notices 81
credit-card facilities 64
creditor payments 60–2, 62
culture change xv
  under compulsory competitive tendering
      32–5

Data Protection Act (1984) 55–6
debt management 83–4
debt recovery 65
decentralising 3–4, 18–25, 103–4
  costs 6
  creditor payments 62
  current problems 20
  definition xiv
  opportunities 21
  risks 22–4
  statutory initiatives 20
decision-making 5–6, 20
direct labour organisations (DLOs) 27, 34

direct revenue funding 139
direct service organisations (DSOs)
  business planning 37–9
  cash flow management 38
  control systems 21
  financial regulations 39–40
  in financial services 121
  ꞲꞲꞲꞲꞲꞲꞲꞲ ꞲꞲ
  information technology (IT) 36–7
  and insurance 38–9
  management structure 90–1
  performance reviews 30–1, 34
  profit targets 32
Directors of Finance *see* chief financial
    officers
District Audit Service 88
District Valuation Office 67, 127

education service 19, 97
electronic fund transfer (BACS) 64
employees *see* staff
employment protection 43
enabling authorities 106
European Regional Development Fund (ERDF)
    82, 105
European Social Fund (ESF) 105
European Union (EU) grants 105
exchequer functions 15–17, 57–71
  Council tax benefits 62–3
  Council tax collection 68–70
  creditor payments 60–2
  future developments 120
  housing benefits 62–3
  income 64–6
  insurance 70–1
  non-domestic rate collection 67–8
  payroll 50, 57–60
  precept payments 69
  risk management 70–1
  superannuation 3, 12, 66–7, 96
  VAT administration 70
external audits 32, 87–9
external funding 81–2
externalisation of financial management 103

final accounts 79
financial planning, *see* planning
financial services 41, 42, 121
fraud 8, 9

gearing 132
GEST (Grants for Education Support and
    Training) 105
goals 2

government
    grants 81–2, 104–5, 128
    influences on capital expenditure 137, 138
    local authority spending controls 117, 126,
        132–3
    subsidies 63
grants 81–2, 104–5, 128
Grants for Education Support and Training
    (GEST) 105
GREA (grant-related expenditure assessment) 128
Greater London Council 126

holiday homes 127
Housing Act (1988) 66
housing benefits 62–3
housing management 41, 42
    rent collection 3, 65

income, *see* revenue
income arrears 16
incremental budgeting 74–5
information systems
    for asset management 91–2
    and decentralisation 24
    and effective management 4, 6, 121–2
    efficiency of 5
    traditional systems 49–52
information technology (IT) 45–56
    and compulsory competitive tendering 37,
        41, 42
    computer security 55
    costs 46, 47
    data protection 55–6
    hardware options 46, 52–3
    local PCs 53, 54
    managing developments in 46–8
    non-compatibility 48
    requirements 48–9
    software options 47, 53
    stand-alone PCs 53–4
insurance 70–1
    and CCT 38–9
    self-insurance 71
internal audits 10, 13–14, 85–7
investment management 4, 94–6
invoice payment 15, 61

leasing 47, 137
legal services 41, 42
legislation
    and capital spending 136, 137
    for capping 133
    and chief financial officers 9–11
    and compulsory competitive tendering
        (CCT) 27

and decentralisation 19–20, 21
and powers to trade 34–5
and superannuation 66, 67
and waste disposal 27
leisure centres 64
Local Authority (Goods and Services) Act
    (1970) 34–5
Local Education Authorities (LEAs) 19, 97
Local Government Act (1972) 10, 11
Local Government Act (1988) 27, 32, 90
Local Government Finance Acts 10, 88, 125
Local Government and Housing Act (1989)
    136, 137
Local Government Planning and Land Act
    . (1980) 27
Local Government Review 104, 106
Local Management of Schools (LMS) 3, 19–20,
    21, 34, 97

management
    achieving effective management 5–6
    definition 1–2
    development 118–19
    restraints 20
    structure 90–1
    total management 19
managers 19, 21
metropolitan councils 126

National Lottery 105
National Parks Supplementary Grant 105
net revenue expenditure 125
Nolan Committee 8
non-domestic rate collection 67–8, 127

objectives
    of audits 85–6, 88
    of management 22
output indicators 98
overheads 12, 107

payroll 50, 57–60
pensions, *see* superannuation administration
performance
    in exchequer functions 15–16
    reviews 23, 98–101, 122
    and service level agreements 111–12
    standards and charters 4
personnel services 41, 42
planning
    business planning 90–1
    business plans 24, 37–8
    strategic plans 72–3
    see also budgets

Index

Police Grant 105, 128
policy decisions 20
poll tax, *see* community charge
precept payments 69
probity 8, 9, 20, 37
  and efficiency 11, 13
profiles of the Audit Commission 88, 99
profiling and budgetary control 76
profit targets 32
project appraisal 89–90
property
  and capital spending 136
  services 41, 92
  valuation 68, 127
public expenditure control 117, 126, 132–3
Public Works Loan Board (PWLB) 83, 84
purchase order systems 60
purchaser/provider split 33, 106

rateable values (RV) 127
rent allowances 62–3
rent collection 3, 65
responsibilities
  of chief financial officers 7–11, 21
  of DSO boards/committees 31
return of expenditure and rates (RER) 80
revenue 125–33
  business rates 67–8, 127
  capping 132–3
  collection and accounting 64–6
  community charge 65, 68, 70, 104, 129–31
  Council tax 81, 104, 131–2
  gearing 132
  grants 81–2, 104–5, 128
  net revenue expenditure 125
  standard spending assessments (SSAs) 81,
    128–9
revenue out-turn/capital out-turn (RO/CO)
  forms 80
revenue spending 135
revenue support grant 104
risks
  analysis 11
  of decentralising 22–4
  management 70–1

salaries, *see* payroll
schools 19, 97
Section 11 Grants 105
security of data 55–6
self-insurance 71
service
  committees 30, 31
  costs 106–8
  quality 44
  times 98
service level agreements (SLA) 97, 108–12,
  113–14, 141–3
service level statements (SLS) 113, 144–5
Shaw classification 88–9
single regeneration budget (SRB) 81, 105
software 47, 53, 55
spending controls 117, 126, 132–3
staff
  numbers 120–1
  resources 47
  retention 119
  review and development 24
standard spending assessments (SSAs) 81,
  128–9
standing orders 24
statutory constraints on borrowing 136
statutory financial returns 80
stop-loss cover 71
strategic plans 72–3
sundry debtors systems 64–5
superannuation 3, 12, 66–7, 96
support services framework 112–13, 144–5
systems auditing 86–7
systems-based auditing 87

teacher training 104–5
total management 19
training 4, 23, 24, 97–8, 119
transaction codes 50–1
transactions auditing 86
Transfer of Undertakings Regulations (TUPE)
  43
transparency 9
Transport Supplementary Grant 105
treasurers *see* chief financial officers

uniform national business rate 67, 127
utilisation rates 98

valuation of property 68, 127
value for money 88, 93–4
VAT administration 70
virements 6, 20, 21, 39, 76
virus-checking software 55

wages, *see* payroll
waste disposal 27
Wednesbury Case 9
white-collar services 41–2

zero-based budgeting 74